# 7 Steps to a Winning Resume

# 7 Steps
## to a Winning Resume

**Carl Lackstrom**

Copyright © 2019 Carl Lackstrom

All rights reserved. No part of this publication may be reproduced, distributed, or transmitted in any form or by any means, including photocopying, recording, or other electronic or mechanical methods, without the prior written permission of the publisher, except in the case of brief quotations embodied in reviews and certain other non-commercial uses permitted by copyright law.

This work is sold with the understanding that the author is not engaged in rendering professional career services. The advice and strategies contained herein may not be suitable for your situation. If expert assistance is required, the service of the appropriate professional should be sought.

While the publisher and author have used their best efforts in preparing this book, they make no representations or warranties with respect to the accuracy or completeness of the contents of this book and accepts no liability of any kind for any losses or damages caused or alleged to be caused, directly or indirectly, from using the information contained in this work.

*For Andrew, Aidan, and Annika*

# Download Your Free LinkedIn Companion Guide

To say thanks for buying my book, I would like to give you The 7 Steps LinkedIn Companion Guide for free!
Go to http://www.BookHip.com/ZWNCPC

# Table of Contents

About the 7 Steps ............................................................................. 1
Before You Start: Read This First .................................................... 3
Step 1: Create Your Career Inventory ............................................ 13
Step 2: Identify Your Professional Value Proposition ................... 23
Step 3: Define Your Target Job ...................................................... 29
Step 4: Draft Your Core Resume Sections .................................... 35
Step 5: Build Your Baseline Resume .............................................. 53
Step 6: Check Your Resume .......................................................... 73
Step 7: Customize Your Baseline Resume .................................... 79
Alternative Resume Formats ......................................................... 85
Some Final Winning Resume Tips .............................................. 101
Beyond the Winning Resume ...................................................... 105
About the Author ......................................................................... 107

# About the 7 Steps

Job hunting is hard. It's usually a numbers game. The more people you network with, the more visible you make yourself to recruiters and hiring companies, and the more jobs you apply for, the greater your chances of success. But, at the same time, you are competing against hundreds or even thousands of people for the same opportunities.

There is a lot of advice out there on how to conduct a job search. Some of this advice is good; some of it's bad. A lot of job search guidance tells you what to do, or how things should look, but it doesn't explain very well *how* to do it. It's a challenge just figuring out where to start. You can spend a lot of time and effort just sorting the good from the bad.

It may be time you don't have. If you have a job, your time is already taken up by work, family, and all the other things in your life. If you are out of work you don't have time to waste and want to get your job search started as quickly as possible.

As a result, many people don't master the basics they need for an effective job search because they don't have the time or patience, or they can't sort through all the conflicting advice.

However, if you master the basics, you can improve your position in the job market and accelerate your job search. To be successful, you don't have to be perfect; you just have to be better than the competition. And even with just the basics, you can place yourself ahead of most job seekers and increase your chances of getting the job you want.

I want to make it a little easier for you.

*7 Steps to a Winning Resume* will give you the tools to create a critical part of a successful job search: your resume.

Throughout the *7 Steps*, I give you simple directions and exercises to follow, along with straightforward explanations, examples, tips, and checklists. I strip out the information you don't need and focus you on mastering the basics of writing a resume.

Are you ready?

Let's get started!

# Before You Start
## Read This First

There are several reasons why you might need a resume:

- You are looking for a new job.
- A recruiter contacted you about a new opportunity.
- You need one for networking.
- You want to freshen up an old resume "just in case."

Whatever your reason, creating an *winning* resume can be difficult and time-consuming.

This 7 **Step** guide is designed to make writing a winning resume easier and quicker. It provides practical information and exercises that focus your effort so you use your time efficiently. The 7 **Steps** will help you master resume basics that will put you ahead of your competition and help you get the job you want.

Before we get to the practical details, let's review some key questions about resumes and the 7 **Steps**. The answers will help you better understand the practical exercises and make them easier to complete.

## What Is a Resume?

As you read this, you are probably thinking you already know what a resume is.

Think again.

Many people believe that their resume is about them, that it's supposed to be a summary of their personal experience and achievements.

This is the wrong way to think.

Instead, your resume *must* be about *what you can do for a new employer*.

Simply put, your resume is a sales tool. Despite many of the recent changes to the job search process, your resume continues to be the core document you use to sell yourself to potential employers.

Your resume must clearly communicate the *results* you have delivered for past employers and how you can do the same for someone else.

## How Do I Use My Resume?

You usually use a resume in one of four ways:

- You use it to apply for a job.
- You share it with networking contacts.
- You make it available to recruiters, either by posting it online or sending it to them directly.
- You use it to build other job search and networking tools, such as your LinkedIn profile.

> ## *Winning Resume Tip*
>
> You will have other tools to market yourself to potential employers, such as your LinkedIn or other online profiles, personal web pages, a portfolio, and so on, but you must make sure they are all consistent with your resume.

## *Who or What Reviews My Resume?*

There are four main types of reviewers: applicant tracking systems, recruiters, decision makers, and networking contacts.

A bit more about each:

*Applicant tracking systems (ATS).* These are software systems employers use to manage their recruiting processes. An ATS can post open positions online, process online applications, screen resumes for suitability, track interviews, and process job offers. Chances are, if you have applied for a job online, you have used an ATS.

*Recruiters.* Recruiters identify and screen potential candidates for an organization's open positions. Recruiters can be internal or external to the hiring company. You may end up dealing with both for the same position.

*Decision makers.* These are the people who decide whether to hire you or not. This group will always include the hiring manager but can also include others, such as senior management or potential colleagues.

*Networking contacts.* Networking contacts are people you give your resume to in the hope that they will connect you with other people and job opportunities.

## *What Do Reviewers Want and How Do They Look at My Resume?*

Each type of reviewer has different objectives when reading your resume and will look at it in different ways.

*ATS.* A primary function of an ATS is to determine if your experience is a match for the skills and qualifications listed in the job description. An ATS does this to narrow down the number of resumes a person has to review. It will automatically screen your resume for things like your job titles, dates of employment, skills, and keywords and phrases from the job description. Typically, an ATS will score, or rank, your resume on how well it matches the job requirements. If your resume has a high enough score, the system will mark it for further review. If your resume has a low score, the system will not move it forward.

*Recruiters.* A recruiter needs to qualify or disqualify your resume for evaluation by decision makers. A recruiter wants to present decision makers with resumes that are a good match for the open position. Even if an ATS prescreens, a recruiter will still need to review a number of resumes. To select resumes for further review, a recruiter tries to answer the following questions as quickly as possible:

- Does the resume show the applicant has the necessary skills, experience, and background for the job opening?
- Are there reasons why I should reject this person?
    - Resume errors (spelling, punctuation, etc.)
    - Resume badly formatted
    - Resume content unclear and difficult to understand
    - Applicant does not live in the area
    - Employment gaps
    - Lack of required education

To answer these questions, the recruiter starts by scanning, usually ***in less than ten seconds***, your resume for the following:

- Name
- Contact information
- Present location
- Current/previous employers

- Current/previous job titles
- Dates of employment
- Education
- Listed skills

If your resume passes the initial scan, the recruiter *may* spend more time looking at its details. At the end of the review, the recruiter will either forward your resume to a decision maker or discard it.

*Decision makers.* A decision maker's initial objective is the same as that of a recruiter: to see if you have the appropriate skills, experience, and background for the job opening. But the decision maker is also trying to answer, at least subconsciously, questions such as:

- What can this person do for me?
- Will this person help me, or my team, be successful?
- Can this person help solve my/our problems?
- Does this person work well with others?
- Will this person be a good fit for my team and the organization?

Decision makers also will start by quickly scanning (in less than ten seconds) your resume to understand your background. If they are satisfied that you meet the basic job requirements, they may review your resume in more detail.

From this point on, decision makers are trying to determine *what you can do for them and their organization*. If your resume demonstrates how you can provide value, especially in comparison with other candidates, then you are likely on your way to an interview.

*Networking contacts.* Networking contacts have different objectives from those of other reviewers. Unless you are lucky, they are not assessing your fit for a position they have open. Instead, they are trying to answer the following:

- What has this person done in the past and how do they demonstrate what they can do for an employer?
- Are there any recommendations I can make to this person about their resume or job search?
- Whom do I know who might be able to help this person?
- Whom do I know who has a need or problem that this person might be able to solve?
- Would giving this person's resume to someone I know make me look bad, by association?

Networking contacts, particularly if you know them well, are more likely to take the time to review your resume in detail. However, the initial few seconds of their review is still critical. During this time, they make an initial judgment about whether they would be comfortable passing your resume on to others.

## What Is a Winning Resume?

A winning resume demonstrates, **better than other candidates' resumes**, how you can deliver results for a future employer, and how your skills and experiences match the requirements for a specific position. It provides clear information structured in ways that make it easy for the systems and people reviewing your resume to find answers to their questions.

Ultimately, a winning resume is one that motivates your reader to move you forward in the hiring process, invite you to an interview, or recommend you to another person. To accomplish this, a winning resume must be:

*Focused.* Your resume must communicate the results you have delivered to previous employers and communicate your relevant skills and experience for the specific job you are pursuing.

*Concise.* Your resume must contain just enough information to interest the readers and make them want to interview you or take the next step in the hiring process.

*Easy to read.* Your resume format must make it easy for readers to scan and find the information they want to see.

*Error-free.* Your resume must be free of any content, format, or punctuation mistakes.

*Truthful.* Your resume must provide information that you can corroborate with your experience.

## *Will a Winning Resume Guarantee Me an Interview?*

In short, no.

There are a lot of factors that determine whether you land an interview, let alone a job.

Your goal for your resume should be for the reader to advance you to the next step in the hiring process. A well-constructed, effective resume will significantly improve the chances of that happening and ultimately increase your invitations for an interview. And the more interviews you get, the less time you will spend searching for a job.

But even a winning resume won't get you an interview if your skills and experience are not a match for a company's requirements. For example, if you are a computer programmer applying for HR jobs chances are you are not going to get a lot of interviews. If you lack relevant experience it won't matter how good your resume is. Don't waste your time; be sure your experiences and skills are in line with the job description.

Still, one thing is sure. A poorly constructed resume will certainly keep you from getting interviews, even if you are qualified for the jobs you are pursuing.

A strong, effective resume is a necessity for a successful job search.

## *How Do I Write a Winning Resume?*

There is no one right way to write a winning resume.

Everyone reviewing a resume looks for different things and reacts differently to what they read. Furthermore, everyone has unique skills and experiences that make their resume different from anyone else's. What might be a winning resume in some circumstances might not be a winner in others.

The fact that there are a variety of resume formats and styles you can use just makes it more difficult. Furthermore, the variety of views and advice on resume writing is extensive. Some of it's good and some of it's bad.

So, what to do?

The good news is that you can deliver a successful resume, in most situations, by simply focusing on the five basic characteristics of a winning resume:

- Focused
- Easy to read
- Concise
- Error-free
- Truthful

The **7 Steps** focus on these characteristics to ensure you write the effective resume you need.

Remember, you are not trying to be perfect—just better than your competition.

## *What Is More Important for a Resume: Good Layout, or Strong Content?*

Good layout and strong content are both equally important. You cannot have a winning resume with one and not the other.

Well-formatted resumes are easy to read; reviewers can easily locate the information they want to see. If formatted correctly, a good resume layout can provide the leverage you need to position yourself at the top of the applicant pool. If the formatting is unclear, you run the risk of a reviewer quickly discarding your resume.

While a good layout may help get you through the first few seconds of a review, without content that is focused and concise your resume will still find its way into the discard pile. You must have strong content that illustrates how your skills, experience, and achievements make you an excellent fit for the target job. Your content must also be concise enough to have an impact on your readers in a short amount of time, making them want to learn more about you, preferably through an interview.

## How Long Will It Take Me to Write a Winning Resume?

How long will depend on various factors, including how much experience you have.

If you work through the 7 **Steps** nonstop, writing your resume should take at least a half to a full day. You may want or need to spread the **Steps** out over several days.

As you will see, I recommend you take breaks at certain points to refresh yourself and your perspective. You may also find your focus during exercises improved if you complete the exercise steps over a reasonable period.

Ultimately, you should go at a pace that supports your current job search situation. If you must complete a resume in short order, then push on through.

## Will This Guide Help Me If I Already Have a Resume?

Absolutely.

If you need to update your current resume, you will still find it useful to go through each of the **Steps**. The good news is that with an existing resume, you should already have some of the material you need to complete the exercises.

## How is This Guide Structured?

As mentioned at the beginning, **this section** provides key information you need to know before starting.

**Steps 1, 2 & 3** take you through exercises that help you develop the basic information and content you need to build your resume.

**Steps 4, 5 & 6** take you through the construction of a baseline resume that will position you for your target job.

**Step 7** shows you how to customize your baseline resume for specific jobs.

The guide's last two sections cover alternative resume formats and provide some final resume tips you might find useful.

## *Do I Need to Follow All the Steps in Order?*

No, but I recommend you read the guide all the way through before you decide.

Each **STEP** and the associated exercises build off the previous **STEPS** to help you construct the best possible resume. If you don't complete the steps in order, you may not benefit fully from the exercises.

Still, you may be in a situation where you prefer to pick where to start and what exercises to complete. You can adapt most of the **STEPS** and exercises to whatever plan is best for you.

It's time to move on to the practical exercises.

---

### *Before You Start Checklist: Resume Basics*

At this point, you should understand

- What a resume is and how you use it
- Who or what reviews your resume and what they are looking for
- The five characteristics of a winning resume

If you have missed any of these points, go back and read **this section** again.

# Step 1
## Create Your Career Inventory

For many people, remembering what they did and what they accomplished in any given job is the most difficult part of writing a resume. If you are like me, you can probably write a basic description of your previous jobs, but you have a hard time remembering details about specific responsibilities, projects, or accomplishments.

Creating a Career Inventory will help you remember and document important job information. It becomes a detailed outline of your professional experience and provides the raw material you need to write your resume.

Although we do not cover it directly in this guide, your Career Inventory can also provide useful information for other parts of your job search including the following:

- Identifying career examples and stories for use during interviews
- Completing formal job applications
- Identifying people who can act as references or provide testimonials
- Negotiating salary and benefits

> *Winning Resume Tip*
>
> You should create a Career Inventory even if you are just revising an existing resume. Chances are you will remember valuable details not on your current resume or uncover other information useful for your job search.

## Exercise #1
## Create Your Career Inventory

In this exercise, you create an outline of your current and previous jobs. The exercise should take between thirty and ninety minutes, depending on how much experience you have.

### *Exercise Step 1: Preparation*

Sit where you can work without distractions. Have pen, pencil, paper, note cards, or a computer available to document your inventory. Use whatever works best for you. At some point, you will want to get your Inventory in a word processing or spreadsheet file for easier management.

When completing the remaining exercise steps, remember:

*Do*

- Write down everything you can think of, even if you don't think it is important. You never know what might be useful.

- Quantify information whenever possible (e.g., number of people, $ amounts, % changes, total numbers, etc.).

- Take a break if you need to. It can be difficult to remember details from previous jobs. Don't frustrate and exhaust yourself. Just remember to come back and finish.

*Don't*

- Worry about grammar, writing style, or format. Just capture your information in whatever way is easiest (e.g., bullet points, sentence fragments, short descriptions, etc.).
- Spend too much time on things you can't remember. Make a note and move on. Come back and update your inventory when you have the details.

The goal of this exercise is to list as much information as you can. Think of it as a brainstorming exercise where you quickly try to remember as much as possible.

Don't get bogged down trying to remember every detail of your previous jobs. If you get stuck, move on.

## *Exercise Step 2: Job List*

Create a list of your current and previous jobs. Go back as far as you want, but include your positions for at least the last fifteen years. If you do not have fifteen years of experience, go back as far as you can. Consider including both paying jobs and volunteer work.

For each position, document:

- Your title
- Organization name
- Location where you worked (city and state)
- Dates you held position (month and year)
- Supervisor name(s) and title(s)
- Other key contacts at organization (coworkers, senior management, etc.)
- Company website address
- Organization contact phone number (if you don't remember the number, look online at the company's website)

- Salary and major benefits (base salary, bonus, 401k, vacation time, health insurance, company vehicle, etc.)

Don't spend too much time on these items if you don't have all the information. Do what you can now and complete the remaining items later.

After you have documented your basic job information, leave space under each position for later exercise steps. Create the following sections but don't try to complete them right now:

- Job Responsibilities
- Results/Achievements
- Skills

Once you have listed all your jobs, move on to the next exercise step.

> ## Winning Resume Tip
>
> Some of the information you collect, such as supervisors' names, contact numbers, and so on, is not necessary for your resume. But you will be glad you have it when you fill out job applications, complete background check documentation, or provide information in other parts of the hiring process.

## Exercise Step 3: Job Responsibilities

Create a job responsibilities section for your current, or most recent, job. List and describe all your job responsibilities. Don't get hung up trying to write a job description. Just list the information in the easiest way possible (e.g., bullet points, sentence fragments, short descriptions). You will write more formal job descriptions later.

Some key items you may want to list:

- Scope of responsibilities

- Things you did on a day-to-day basis to perform your job
- Number of people or size of organization supervised (if any)
- Size of budget (if any)
- Size of territory covered
- List of projects managed or worked on
- Situation you faced when starting job
- Any information that provides context about your job responsibilities

Once you are satisfied with this section, move on to the next exercise step.

## Exercise Step 4: Results/Achievements

Create a results/achievements section for your current, or most recent, job. List, describe, and quantify all the results you delivered to your organization.

Examples of results/achievements you might want to list:

- Increased sales or revenue
- Cost savings
- Improved organizational or staff performance
- Increased productivity
- Improved quality
- Process improvements
- Increased customer satisfaction
- Completed projects
- Developed new organizational capabilities
- Reduced errors
- Reduced risk

- Any other identifiable results you achieved for your employer

Since one of the goals of your resume is to showcase the results you have delivered, you need to provide as much detail and context about them as possible. When listing your results, make sure you describe the following for each of them:

- The situation or challenge you faced
- The actions you took
- The results and benefits your actions delivered

To complete this section, list any awards or official recognition you might have received. Examples:

- Employee awards (e.g., employee of the month/year, and/or awards for excellence)
- Performance rankings (e.g., top sales performer in region)
- Team awards

When you have captured as many results and achievements as possible, move on to the next exercise step.

## *Exercise Step 5: Skills*

Create a skills section for your current/most recent job. List any specific skills that you learned or utilized during your time in this position.

Focus on identifying skills that were directly relevant to your job responsibilities. Remember skills can either be hard or soft skills.

Make sure you identify in this section any IT skills, software, and systems you may have used in your job.

## Exercise Step 6: Complete Exercise Steps 3-5 for All Jobs in Your Inventory

Move on to your next most recent job and repeat Exercise Steps 3-5. Continue to repeat the exercise steps until you have listed job descriptions, results/achievements, and skills for each of the jobs on your inventory list.

## Exercise Step 7: Education and Training

Create a new section for your education and training. List your degrees and any training programs you have completed. For each of your degrees or training programs, try to capture:

- Name of degree, certificate, or training
- Name and location of school or training program
- Major or course of study
- Dates of attendance and graduation (if applicable)
- GPA (if applicable)
- Academic awards
- Key advisors or teachers

Feel free to include additional information. You probably will not use all this information on your resume, but you may find it helpful at other points during your job search.

## Exercise Step 8: Additional Inventory Sections

Depending on your experience, you may find it useful to add additional inventory sections detailing other types of career information. Possible sections:

- Volunteer activities (if you have not already included these in your list of jobs)
- Articles, papers, or books you have written

- Public speaking engagements or professional presentations
- Professional or industry awards

Use your judgment on what additional inventory sections to include. If you think the information might be useful for your resume, or job search in general, then go ahead and include it in the inventory.

## Exercise Step 9: Take a Break

Once you have fully documented all your jobs, take a break, and congratulate yourself! You have completed your Career Inventory, one of the most important steps to building a winning resume.

Put your Career Inventory aside for a little while, and then come back for **Exercise Step 10**.

## Exercise Step 10: Review and Update

Review your Career Inventory and update the information as you see fit. You may have remembered additional information, or you may want to revise what you documented in the different sections.

Make sure you go back and research any details you may not have been able to complete initially.

---

### Winning Resume Tip

Your Career Inventory is something you should update and maintain on a periodic basis. Every six months or so, sit down and update your current job information. Focus on listing new results/achievements, responsibilities, and skills. Periodic updates to your Career Inventory will make it easier, and quicker, for you to revise your resume the next time you need to.

---

Good work! Now that you have finished your Career Inventory, it is time to move on to the next **Step**.

*Step 1 Checklist: Career Inventory*

In **Step 1**, you should have:

- Created a Career Inventory that captures information on all your previous jobs, including your job responsibilities, results and achievements, and skills
- Listed all your education and training
- Included any useful additional information in your Career Inventory
- Reviewed and updated your inventory with any information you forgot or did not have available initially

If you have missed anything, go back, review **Step 1** again, and complete any necessary items.

# Step 2
## Identify Your Professional Value Proposition

Now you will use your Career Inventory to help identify what you are good at and what makes you uniquely valuable to an employer. You will do this by defining your professional value proposition (PVP).

Your PVP is a focused outline of the skills and experiences that are common to your career. It will help you write a resume that quickly demonstrates your value to an employer. Demonstrating this value is critical to capturing your readers' attention within the first few seconds of their review. Your PVP will include

- A list of common elements across your career
- A list of your key skills
- A list of why you are good at what you do
- One or more PVP statements that concisely communicate what you can do for an employer

Let's move on to the exercise.

# Exercise #2
# Identify Your PVP

The goal of this exercise is to create an outline of the common skills, experiences, and achievements that make up your PVP. This exercise should take between thirty and sixty minutes, depending on how many jobs you have had.

## *Exercise Step 1: Preparation*

Sit where you can work without distractions. Have your Career Inventory as well as pen, pencil, paper, note cards, or computer available. Use whatever is most comfortable to initially document your PVP. As you did with your Career Inventory, you will want to get your PVP in a word processing or spreadsheet file for easier management.

When documenting your PVP, you are not trying to write polished content. Don't get hung up on grammar, style, or format. Focus on capturing the important information in a way that is easy for you to use (e.g., bullet points, sentence fragments, short descriptions).

## *Exercise Step 2: Identify Common Elements in Your Career Inventory*

Review your Career Inventory. Look across your job history. Identify and make a list of common elements related to the positive results you provided for your employer(s).

Elements to consider include

- Roles and responsibilities
- Skills
- Experiences
- Types of results
- Methods of delivering results
- Industries

- Types of customer or client
- Positive ways you interact with and manage people
- Company size
- Professional interests
- IT system experience

Don't be limited to just these elements. If you see something that is consistent across your career, or you think is key, make it part of your list.

## *Exercise Step 3: Consolidate Your List of Key Skills*

Starting with the information from **Exercise Step 2**, create a separate list of your key skills. You should already have listed various skills as part of your Career Inventory under each of your jobs. Simply review those skills, identify the key ones, and place them in a new consolidated list.

List as many skills as you can. Try to come up with at least nine to twelve key skills but don't limit yourself if you can list more.

If you have multiple IT related skills, you may want to have two sections in your list:

- Professional skills (general)
- IT skills

Do a last check to make sure you have captured all your relevant skills.

## *Exercise Step 4: Identify What Makes You Good at What You Do*

Review the list of common career elements and skills you created in the previous exercise steps and ask yourself the following questions:

- What are the things I do well?
- What makes me good at what I do?
- What do other people think makes me good at what I do?

- What are the skills or traits that have made me successful in my jobs?

Create a list of all the things you can think of. Make sure you particularly list the qualities that have helped make you successful in your different jobs.

## Exercise Step 5: Create PVP Statements

Now it's time to put everything together. A PVP statement is a concise statement of one to three sentences that summarizes what you can do for an employer. Look at all the things you listed in the previous exercise steps. Based on what you see, ask yourself:

- What kind of results do I consistently deliver?
- How do I deliver these results?
- To whom have I delivered these results?
- Under what conditions have I delivered these results?

Using your answers to these questions, write one or more PVP statements. Here are some example formats:

- I provide (type of results) to (type of company, industry, client, etc.) by (type of actions).
- I deliver (type of results) to (type of company, industry, client, etc.) by (type of actions).
- I help (type of company, industry, client, etc.) to do (type of work/results) by (type of actions).

You can use different formats if you wish. What is important is that you summarize in each statement the type of results you deliver, whom you deliver them to, and under what conditions.

> *Winning Resume Tip*
>
> You can use your PVP statements for more than one purpose, including the creation of an "elevator speech," which summarizes what you can do for an employer. You can then deliver this "speech" to people you meet professionally or during your job search.

Let's look at some examples.

## *Exercise Step 5: Examples*

- I deliver increased sales and revenues to companies serving the restaurant and hospitality industries through innovative sales and marketing techniques and focused account management.

- I help companies realize the full benefits of their enterprise projects and system implementations by creating and managing high-performing, integrated, project teams that deliver on time and budget.

- I maximize organizational performance and reduce risk in customer-facing financial institutions by transforming operations through process improvement, control implementation, and staff training.

Don't be afraid to draft different PVP statements. Try them out and see which ones best summarize what you can provide employers.

If you are satisfied with your statements, then you have finished the exercise and are ready to move on to **Step 3**.

Remember all the materials you developed in this exercise combine to make up your overall PVP. You will use it to good effect, starting in **Step 4**.

## Step 2 Checklist: PVP

In **Step 2**, you should have:

- Identified common elements in your career
- Created a list of your common skills
- Identified what makes you good at what you do
- Created PVP statements

If you have missed anything, go back, review **Step 2** again, and complete any necessary items.

# Step 3
## Define Your Target Job

To write a winning resume, you must have some idea of what kind of job you want. There are thousands of different positions, all requiring different skills and experience for success.

Your target job could be of several different types:

- It's similar to your current job, or a job you have done in the past.
- It's a higher-level position in your current career path.
- It's a significantly different type of job, one that you have identified through research and reflection on your interests and experience.

A winning resume *focuses* on showing how your skills and experience match those of your target job. This focus requires more than just knowing what kind of work you want to do. It also requires you to define the common skills and experience necessary for the position. The next exercise helps you do this.

# Exercise #3
# Define Your Target Job Requirements and Keywords

Your objective in this exercise is to identify key skills, experiences, and qualifications commonly required for your target job. You will want to save the material you develop in the exercise in a separate document.

As usual, sit where you can work without distractions and use whatever is most comfortable to document your target job.

## Exercise Step 1: Find Target Job Descriptions

Using the basic title of your target job, search online job sites to find example job descriptions.

There are numerous sites you can use for your search. Start with the larger job boards such as Indeed.com or SimplyHired.com. When searching for job descriptions consider the following:

- Use variations of your target job title during your search to increase the number of job description results.

- Don't limit your search to a geographic location. Search nationally. (You are just trying to find example job descriptions, not a job in a specific location.)

- Narrow your search to specific industries if it is relevant to your target job and experience.

Depending on your target job, and your initial search results, you may also want to check out niche job boards. There are hundreds of niche job sites out there, so I won't list any here. If you want to find one, simple online searches using keywords such as "list of job boards" or "best job boards for _____," should give you a place to start.

Another source for job descriptions is the O*NET OnLine website, sponsored by the US Department of Labor. It is a database of occupational information that contains hundreds of standardized job descriptions. You can access it at https://www.onetonline.org/.

## Exercise Step 2: Select the Best Job Descriptions for Your Target Job

Chances are you have located various job descriptions in your search. Review them and select one to five descriptions you feel best relate to your target job.

> ### Winning Resume Tip
>
> The total number of descriptions you select does not matter, but I recommend picking at least two to three. Keep the number manageable as well. Selecting too many will make it more difficult to complete the next exercise steps. Use your judgment.

Save your selected descriptions so you can access them later. Don't just bookmark them in your browser. Jobs on boards can drop offline if they expire or are filled by the posting company. Save descriptions by saving the complete web page, taking a screenshot, or cutting and pasting the description into a word processing document.

## Exercise Step 3: Identify Common Job Requirements

Review the job descriptions you selected. Identify and list the common elements required for all the job descriptions including:

- Responsibilities
- Skills (both hard and soft)
- Experience
- Levels of education or certification
- Other required qualifications

As you did for your Career Inventory and PVP, you should be documenting these common elements in whatever way works best for you.

## Exercise Step 4: Identify Keywords for Your Target Job

Along with common job requirements, you should identify common keywords or phrases associated with your selected job descriptions.

Identify and list any keywords or phrases you think are important for your target job.

You may identify some keywords based on your target job's common requirements. Others may suggest themselves as you review the job descriptions.

For the most part, you should be able to find keywords and phrases just by comparing the different job descriptions. But if you need them, various online tools (generally free) can help identify keywords and phrases.

Some tools are designed for web SEO but can still be used to help identify job description keywords. You can find them by doing an online search for "keyword density calculator," "keyword density tools," or "keyword density checker." You will need to enter the job description's web address, or cut and paste the description, into the tool.

Another type of tool you can use is a word-cloud generator. This online tool creates word clouds that highlight the most common keywords and phrases in the content you select. A word-cloud generator can work from web addresses, uploaded files, or from text you cut and paste into the tool. Two popular word cloud generators are www.wordclouds.com and www.wordle.net.

If you use any of these online tools, review the results and pick only those keywords and phrases that are relevant to your target job.

## Exercise Step 5: Identify Target Job Success Factors

Review your example job descriptions and the common requirements and keywords you have identified. List five to ten things you will need, or must do, to make yourself successful in your target job.

When you make your list, focus on the type of result you will have to deliver in your target job. Think about the things that a potential employer would find valuable. Remember to consider soft skill factors, such as leadership, communication, relationship management, teamwork, critical and creative thinking, and so on.

When you have finished listing your target job's success factors, you are ready to move on to the next **Step**.

---

*Step 3 Checklist: Target Job*

In **Step 3**, you should have

- Found and selected the best job descriptions for your target job
- Identified and listed common job requirements and keywords for your target job
- Identified and listed success factors for your target job

If you have missed any, go back, review **Step 3** again, and complete any necessary items.

# Step 4
## Draft Your Core Resume Sections

You are now ready to draft the two core sections of your resume.

*Professional Experience.* This is the list of your current and past jobs, including descriptions of your roles and responsibilities and the results that you delivered.

*Professional Summary.* This is a brief description of your career and your PVP and includes a list of your skills relevant to your target job.

These two sections are the most important parts of your resume. They demonstrate how you can achieve results for an employer.

The bad news is you may find they are the most difficult parts of your resume to write.

The good news is that with the materials from your Career Inventory and your PVP, you should have the content you need to write both sections.

In this **Step**, you will complete two exercises to write your Professional Experience and Professional Summary.

Although it does not come first in your resume, we start with your Professional Experience. The content you write in this section can help you write your Professional Summary.

Remember you are not yet drafting your full resume. You are writing the core sections separately and will put them together with other resume sections in the next **Step**.

You should complete these exercises using a word processing program to make it easier to incorporate the material you develop into your full resume.

At this point, don't be overly concerned about formatting, although the exercises do include some basic layout instructions that will facilitate building your full resume in **Step 5**.

As always, make sure you are in a place where you can work comfortably with minimal distractions for both exercises.

## Exercise #4
## Draft Your Professional Experience

In this exercise, you will draft your Professional Experience, using your Career Inventory as a primary source of information. For each of your jobs you will include

- Name of company
- Location of company
- Position title
- Dates you worked in this position
- Roles and responsibilities summary
- Bullet point summaries of results and achievements

This exercise can take thirty to ninety minutes (or more) depending on the number of jobs you have held. If you are getting tired, distracted, or frustrated when writing this section, stop and take a break.

> ## *Winning Resume Tip*
>
> You should include in Professional Experience all the positions you have held in the last ten to fifteen years. If you have more than fifteen years of experience, you should consider limiting the number of jobs you list in that section. Including more than fifteen years of experience may make you appear overqualified or may lead to discriminatory opinions about your age.

## *Exercise Step 1: Company, Company Location, Dates, and Position Title*

For your present or most recent position, list your position title, the dates you worked at this job, the company worked for, and the location where you worked.

While there are many ways in which you can format each position in your Professional Experience, I recommend you start with the name of the company, in capital letters, aligned with the left margin.

After the company name and a comma, place the city and state in regular font (not capitalized).

On the same line as your company and location, but aligned with the right margin, list your years of employment (e.g., 2012–Present, 2010–2015).

If your tenure at the job is or was less than two years, you may want to consider using a month/year format for your employment dates (e.g., 3/2016–10/2017, Mar. 2016–Oct. 2017). Just remember to be consistent with how you list dates. If you use a month/year format for any of your positions, use it for all of them.

On the next line down, place your title in bold font.

Check out the examples below.

## Exercise Step 1: Examples

| | |
|---|---|
| ACME LIFE INSURANCE COMPANY, Cincinnati, OH<br>**Senior IT Program Manager** | 2012–Present |
| RELIABLE DISTRIBUTORS, Irving, TX<br>**Account Manager** | 2009–2013 |
| NORTH SHORE CARDIOLOGY SPECIALISTS, Salem, MA<br>**Practice Administrator** | 6/2014–Present |
| ARBOR LIFE INSURANCE COMPANY<br>**Quality Assurance Analyst** | 9/2003–6/2008 |

A critical part of this exercise step is to determine what job title you should use. In most cases, the actual title you hold/held should be appropriate. But your title may be company or industry specific and may not accurately reflect your role and responsibilities. As a result, your title may not have as great an impact on the reader. If you are in this situation, it's okay to consider modifying your title.

You have four basic options:

- You can use your actual title.
- You can simplify your actual title.
- You can use a functional title that better reflects your roles and responsibilities.
- You can combine your actual title with a functional title.

Ultimately, you want your position title to be as relevant as possible for your target job. Just remember a winning resume must be *truthful,* so you should only modify your position title if your changes can be backed up by your actual role, responsibilities, and experience in that job.

> ## *Winning Resume Tip*
>
> If you held more than one position for the same company, you will need to adjust your formatting when you add those jobs to your Professional Experience.
>
> Start by placing your company, location, and overall dates of employment on the first line, as usual.
>
> On the next line, place the title of your most recent job (in bold font). Additionally, place the dates you held that position, aligned with the right margin, in regular font.
>
> For each subsequent job with that company, start with your job title (in bold) and then list the dates you held that position. You will not need to list the company name or location again. Example:
>
> | | |
> |---|---:|
> | PCA NATIONAL BANK, Dallas, TX | 2008–2017 |
> | **Assistant Vice President - Consumer Banking** | 2014–2017 |
> | **Project Manager, Organizational Readiness** | 2012–2014 |
> | **District Manager** | 2010–2012 |
> | **Branch Manager** | 2008–2010 |
>
> Remember you will be adding the job description and the results/achievements bullet points for each position, so make sure you have sufficient space between each position on your actual resume. See the full resumes at the end of this **Step** for examples.

## *Exercise Step 2: Role and Responsibilities Summary*

For your present or most recent position, write a two- to three-sentence summary of your role and responsibilities.

Begin by reviewing your Career Inventory for this position. Use the role and responsibility information you listed in the inventory to help you write your summary.

> ### Winning Resume Tip
>
> Write your summary and the associated results/achievements bullet points in the present tense for your current job. Write the summary and bullet points in the past tense for all previous jobs. You do not need to use a subject in your sentences. To understand this tip, check the exercise and full resume examples.

Don't get stuck trying to provide too much detail about your roles and responsibilities. You need to be concise. Provide just enough information so your readers will have a basic understanding of your job.

Do, however, provide any relevant context about your role and responsibilities. Context can include such things as:

- Size of your company or department (number of people, revenues, budget, number of systems, etc.)
- Scope of your responsibilities
- Size of territory covered
- Number of people you directly supervised
- Number of projects you managed
- The situation when you entered the role (e.g., your position was expected to address a specific challenge or issue)

> ### Winning Resume Tip
>
> Try to avoid the use of industry-specific jargon or acronyms on your resume. Chances are they will be misunderstood and may just confuse your readers. You can make exceptions for keywords or phrases directly related to your target job.

## *Exercise Step 2: Examples*

**Senior IT Program Manager**

Leads enterprise system implementation programs for Fortune 500 Life Insurance Company with $43B in assets. Manages $25M program budget and 20+ program staff. Oversees vendor relationships with key offshore development partners.

**Assistant Vice President - Consumer Banking**

Managed regional retail sales and operations division encompassing 50+ branches across North Texas. Administered multimillion-dollar expense budget. Ensured proper functioning of day-to-day branch operations including vault duties, cash level management, over/short cash controls, and fraud prevention. Coordinated all federal and internal audit activities in branches.

## *Exercise Step 3: Results and Achievements*

For your present or most recent position, create three to five bullet points, each summarizing a specific result you achieved. From the results/achievements section of your Career Inventory select the most significant results and achievements appropriate for your target job. Review your target job's skills and experience requirements you identified to help determine which of your results and achievements are most relevant.

Your bullet points should include at least two core elements:

- The specific result you achieved or value you provided
- The actions you took to achieve the result

To strengthen the bullet points, you can also include contextual information on the challenge or situation you faced when delivering the result.

When writing the bullet points, you can place the core elements in whatever order makes sense. But whenever possible, you should start your bullet points with the results you achieved. Bringing your results to the forefront will help capture the attention of your readers when they quickly scan your resume.

You should always try to quantify the results described in your bullet points, although that may not be possible for all achievements.

Don't be afraid to use general descriptions of your results where necessary. In the right context, they can be just as powerful as quantified results, and may be more appropriate.

Make sure you review the target job keywords and phrases you identified in **Step 4** and try to include some of them in your bullet points if possible.

## Exercise Step 3: Examples

- Drove 22% improvement in customer satisfaction ratings through successful agile development and deployment of new customer account mobile app suite.

- Led $5M cloud migration of 110 applications and 500 system processes to cloud provider over 10-month period resulting in a 26% reduction in IT operational costs.

- Improved territory profitability by 12%, with no loss of mortgage volume by closing and consolidating 3 underperforming branches in the Dallas area.

- Drove 50% growth in national accounts by spearheading effort to target restaurant and hotel chains headquartered in region through strategic account planning, the development of tailored marketing collateral, and enhanced sales presentations.

- Reduced average software project delivery time by 17% by developing and providing agile development training to IT project management staff.

- Increased regional revenues by 22% for restaurant services company by reorganizing sales territory and shifting focus to selling multiservice packages to key accounts.

When describing your experience, you should use different action verbs and adjectives throughout your resume. Overuse of the same words in your bullet points, and in your job descriptions, will limit the impact they have on your resume reader.

You can easily find lists of action verbs and adjectives through an online search. Simply type in "action verbs for resumes" or "resume adjectives" into your search engine, and you should come up with several lists.

You can also use a thesaurus at any point if you need to try to find an alternative word. Your word processing program may have a built-in one, or you can find one online (e.g., www.thesaurus.com).

The following are sample lists for your use.

# Example action verbs

| | | | |
|---|---|---|---|
| *absorbed* | *awarded* | *consolidated* | *directed* |
| *accelerated* | *blocked* | *constructed* | *discovered* |
| *achieved* | *boosted* | *consulted* | *dispatched* |
| *acquired* | *briefed* | *controlled* | *documented* |
| *administered* | *budgeted* | *converted* | *drafted* |
| *advanced* | *built* | *conveyed* | *drove* |
| *advised* | *calculated* | *convinced* | *earned* |
| *advocated* | *campaigned* | *coordinated* | *edited* |
| *affirmed* | *capitalized* | *corresponded* | *educated* |
| *aided* | *centralized* | *counseled* | *enabled* |
| *aligned* | *certified* | *created* | *enforced* |
| *allocated* | *chaired* | *critiqued* | *engineered* |
| *amplified* | *charted* | *cultivated* | *enhanced* |
| *analyzed* | *checked* | *customized* | *ensured* |
| *applied* | *clarified* | *decreased* | *established* |
| *appraised* | *coached* | *deducted* | *evaluated* |
| *approved* | *co-authored* | *defined* | *examined* |
| *arbitrated* | *collaborated* | *delegated* | *exceeded* |
| *arranged* | *communicated* | *delivered* | *executed* |
| *assembled* | *competed* | *demonstrated* | *expanded* |
| *assessed* | *completed* | *designed* | *expedited* |
| *attained* | *composed* | *determined* | *explored* |
| *audited* | *concluded* | *developed* | *fabricated* |
| *authored* | *conferred* | *devised* | *facilitated* |
| *authorized* | *conserved* | *diagnosed* | *fielded* |

| | | | |
|---|---|---|---|
| *focused* | *inspected* | *mobilized* | *promoted* |
| *forecasted* | *inspired* | *modified* | *promoted* |
| *forged* | *instituted* | *monitored* | *prospected* |
| *formalized* | *integrated* | *motivated* | *proved* |
| *formed* | *interpreted* | *navigated* | *publicized* |
| *formulated* | *introduced* | *negotiated* | *qualified* |
| *fostered* | *investigated* | *observed* | *quantified* |
| *founded* | *itemized* | *obtained* | *reached* |
| *funded* | *justified* | *operated* | *received* |
| *furthered* | *launched* | *orchestrated* | *recommended* |
| *gained* | *learned* | *organized* | *reconciled* |
| *generated* | *lectured* | *originated* | *recruited* |
| *guided* | *led* | *outpaced* | *redesigned* |
| *handled* | *lessened* | *outperformed* | *reduced* |
| *headed* | *lifted* | *overhauled* | *refined* |
| *helped* | *listened* | *oversaw* | *refocused* |
| *hired* | *lobbied* | *participated* | *regulated* |
| *identified* | *maintained* | *partnered* | *rehabilitated* |
| *illustrated* | *managed* | *persuaded* | *remodeled* |
| *implemented* | *manipulated* | *pioneered* | *reorganized* |
| *improved* | *mapped* | *planned* | *replaced* |
| *incorporated* | *mapped* | *presented* | *represented* |
| *increased* | *marketed* | *prevented* | *reserved* |
| *indexed* | *maximized* | *prioritized* | *resolved* |
| *influenced* | *measured* | *processed* | *restored* |
| *informed* | *mentored* | *produced* | *restructured* |
| *initiated* | *merged* | *programmed* | *retrieved* |

| | | | |
|---|---|---|---|
| *revamped* | *simplified* | *supported* | *unified* |
| *reviewed* | *solved* | *surpassed* | *united* |
| *revitalized* | *spearheaded* | *surveyed* | *updated* |
| *screened* | *specialized* | *sustained* | *upgraded* |
| *scrutinized* | *standardized* | *targeted* | *valued* |
| *secured* | *stimulated* | *taught* | *verified* |
| *seized* | *streamlined* | *tested* | *volunteered* |
| *selected* | *strengthened* | *tracked* | *wrote* |
| *served* | *succeeded* | *traded* | *yielded* |
| *shaped* | *suggested* | *trained* | |
| *shared* | *supervised* | *transacted* | |
| *showcased* | *supplied* | *transformed* | |

# Example Adjectives

| | | | |
|---|---|---|---|
| *accomplished* | *attentive* | *comprehensive* | *dedicated* |
| *accurate* | *businesslike* | *concerned* | *dependable* |
| *active* | *calculating* | *conscientious* | *detailed* |
| *adaptable* | *calm* | *consistent* | *detail-oriented* |
| *adept* | *capable* | *constructive* | *determined* |
| *advanced* | *charming* | *controlled* | *devoted* |
| *aggressive* | *cheerful* | *cooperative* | *diligent* |
| *agile* | *clear* | *cordial* | *diplomatic* |
| *alert* | *coherent* | *cost-effective* | *discerning* |
| *amiable* | *cohesive* | *courteous* | *disciplined* |
| *amicable* | *committed* | *creative* | *discreet* |
| *articulate* | *competent* | *cutting-edge* | *diverse* |
| *astute* | *complex* | *decisive* | *driven* |

| | | | |
|---|---|---|---|
| *dynamic* | *influential* | *positive* | *smooth* |
| *earnest* | *ingenious* | *practical* | *sophisticated* |
| *economical* | *innovative* | *precise* | *spirited* |
| *effective* | *insightful* | *proactive* | *steadfast* |
| *efficient* | *instrumental* | *productive* | *step-by-step* |
| *elegant* | *intelligent* | *professional* | *strategic* |
| *energetic* | *inventive* | *proficient* | *strong* |
| *enterprising* | *investigative* | *profitable* | *structured* |
| *enthusiastic* | *keen* | *progressive* | *studious* |
| *exact* | *knowledgeable* | *punctual* | *superior* |
| *experienced* | *logical* | *qualified* | *sustainable* |
| *expert* | *loyal* | *realistic* | *systematic* |
| *extensive* | *methodical* | *reliable* | *talented* |
| *fastidious* | *meticulous* | *resilient* | *team-minded* |
| *first-class* | *motivated* | *resourceful* | *thorough* |
| *flexible* | *multifaceted* | *respectful* | *thoughtful* |
| *fluent* | *novel* | *responsive* | *timely* |
| *focused* | *objective* | *results-driven* | *tireless* |
| *genuine* | *orderly* | *revolutionary* | *unique* |
| *groundbreaking* | *organized* | *robust* | *unprecedented* |
| *harmonious* | *passionate* | *self-reliant* | *vast* |
| *honest* | *patient* | *shrewd* | *versatile* |
| *ideal* | *perceptive* | *significant* | *vigorous* |
| *imaginative* | *persistent* | *sincere* | *well-grounded* |
| *impartial* | *personable* | *skilled* | *wholehearted* |
| *industrious* | *pleasant* | *skillful* | *world-class* |

*Exercise Step 4: Complete Your Professional Experience Section*

Now that you have completed your present or most recent position, repeat **Exercise Steps 1–3** for the remaining jobs you plan to include in your resume.

---

*Winning Resume Tip*

When writing results/achievements bullet points, you may want to list more for your more recent positions than for your older jobs (10+ years). A good rule of thumb is to have at least three to five bullet points for more recent positions, if possible, and two to three bullet points for older jobs.

As with any rule of thumb, there are always exceptions. For example, you may want to include more bullet points for positions where you had a long tenure or that are directly relevant to your target job, even if those positions were earlier in your career.

Ultimately, you should include the number of bullet points you think will be most impactful, while remaining concise, based on your work history.

---

Satisfied with your Professional Experience? If yes, you are ready to move on to your Professional Summary.

# Exercise #5
# Draft Your Professional Summary

Your Professional Summary is the section at the very top of your resume, just below your name and contact information. It is a key section because it is your first opportunity to catch the attention of your readers as they scan your resume. It should concisely describe your unique value to potential employers and how you deliver results.

Your Professional Summary should contain three main components:

- A professional title
- A three- to five-line summary paragraph highlighting your unique professional value and experience
- A list of your key skills

Expect to spend thirty to ninety minutes on this exercise. As in the previous exercise, if you are getting tired, distracted, or frustrated, stop and take a break.

## *Exercise Step 1: Create Your Professional Title*

Your professional title is a concise description of the type of position you want. You should base it on your target job, but it should also reflect your experience. Your resume title can either be very specific or more general depending on your preference.

Take a few minutes and draft several different versions of your title. Pick the one that you think best represents your target job and experience.

## *Exercise Step 2: Write Your Summary Paragraph*

Review the PVP material you created in **Step 2**, as well as the target job information you identified in **Step 3**. Write a three- to five-line paragraph that summarizes your unique professional value, experience, and suitability for your target job.

Easier said than done, right? You may find writing a summary paragraph to be difficult. Most people have a hard time promoting themselves, let alone doing it concisely in three to five lines.

Let's break this exercise step down a bit. Here are some sub-steps you can follow:

- Identify three to five key value elements from your PVP material that you want to highlight in your summary. The elements you select should be ones that are most effective at communicating your unique professional value.

- Think of three to five adjectives that you can use to label yourself in your summary (e.g., professional, experienced, focused, transformative, dynamic, collaborative, innovative). Check the list of adjective examples in the previous exercise if you need help getting started.
- Consider using a version of your PVP statement(s) in your summary. You will probably have to modify it, but it can give you a very impactful start.
- Review the Professional Experience section you just created. See if there are any new common elements you want to include in your summary that you hadn't already identified in your PVP material.
- Check your defined target job and confirm the summary elements you selected are appropriate and identify keywords you may want to include in your summary.

Once you have identified the key elements you want to include, go ahead and start writing your summary. Don't be afraid to write several draft summaries to see what works best. See the examples below:

> *Winning Resume Tip*
>
> Always write your summary paragraph in the present tense. Look at the examples below.

## Exercise Step 2: Examples

Transformative executive who elevates and improves operations across organizations. Team builder known for increasing sales and profitability, developing staff, and strengthening compliance controls. Specialist in turning around low-performing territories and branches with extensive experience in the consumer banking, mortgage, and insurance industries.

Proactive manager who improves practice profitability, increases patient satisfaction, controls costs, and optimizes practice operations and IT systems. Strategic planner who creates and drives multiyear plans that increase practice competitiveness in the market. Committed team builder who enables physicians, nurses, and support staff to achieve both organizational and individual goals.

## *Exercise Step 3: Create Your Skills Section*

The last part of your Professional Summary is a list of your key skills. Review your Career Inventory and pick nine to fifteen of your key skills. Make sure you select skills that are relevant to your target job. This section is also a good place to include appropriate keywords and phrases.

Your skills section should be just below your summary paragraph. You can include a section title, but it's not necessary. If you use one, possible titles for this section are:

- Key Skills
- Core Competencies
- Professional Strengths
- Management Skills

Or some other combination you think is appropriate.

Check out the draft Professional Summary below.

## *Exercise Steps 1–3: Full Example*

**Senior IT Program and Project Manager**

Dynamic program manager with track record of delivering multimillion-dollar IT initiatives and projects that meet business requirements, on time and budget. Collaborative leader who builds high-performing teams with both business, technical, and international staff. Certified Project Management and Agile Professional who introduces innovative project management techniques to improve project efficiency and effectiveness.

- Project Management Professional (PMP)
- Certified Scrum Professional (CSP)

- Agile Certified Professional (PMI-ACP)
- Software Development Lifecycle
- Budgeting and Forecasting
- Requirements Gathering and Analysis
- Offshore Development
- ERP Systems
- SaaS and Cloud Architecture
- Information Security
- User Training
- Quality Management

When you have completed drafting both your Professional Experience and your Professional Summary, take a moment to give yourself some kudos. You have now drafted two of the most important sections of your resume and can move on to creating your baseline resume.

## Step 4 Checklist: Core Resume Sections

In **Step 4**, you should have:

- Drafted your Professional Experience covering all your relevant jobs, including a summary of roles and responsibilities and a list of results and achievements for each job
- Drafted your Professional Summary, including a professional title, a summary paragraph, and a list of your key skills

If you have missed anything, go back, review **Step 4** again, and complete any necessary items.

# Step 5
## Build Your Baseline Resume

Now it's time to put all the pieces together.

Your baseline resume is the starting point for any other resumes you may create. It is designed to position you for the target job you defined in **Step 3**.

You can post your baseline resume to a job board, send it to recruiters, or share it with others when networking.

You will also customize this resume when you are applying for specific jobs. (Covered later in **Step 7**.)

Before moving on to the exercise, let's discuss resume formats and layouts.

### *Resume Formats*

There are three basic resume formats:

*Chronological.* A chronological resume usually starts with a brief Professional Summary, with the bulk of the resume being a chronological description of previous jobs.

*Functional.* A functional resume highlights specific skills, abilities, and experiences in an expanded summary section. It downplays work history and may only provide limited details about previous jobs.

*Hybrid.* A hybrid resume contains a combination of chronological and functional elements. It may have an expanded summary section to highlight specific skills and abilities but also contain a reasonable chronological summary of work history.

For most people with experience, the chronological resume is the best option. It is the type of resume most people reviewing your resume will expect to see. The next exercise uses the chronological resume structure to build your baseline resume.

If you are a new graduate, looking for a new career, or returning to the workforce, you may want to use a different resume format. We address alternative resumes later in this Guide. Fortunately, the material you have already developed gives you material you can use in any resume format.

## *Resume Layouts*

There are many different resume layouts you can use successfully. An online search will provide multiple templates to choose from.

For your baseline resume, we will use a basic layout that is simple, clean, and easy to read. But you should feel free to use another layout if you have a preference. Just remember, your resume must be *easy to read* to be a winning resume.

The best way to make your resume easy to read is to keep your layout simple and limit the use of any special formatting or features.

Regardless of layout, there are some basic formatting guidelines you should consider.

### *Fonts*

There are many different fonts available, but only a limited number are suitable for resumes. Any font you use must be easy to read and professional looking.

I recommend using Calibri if you are working with MS Word. It is MS Word's default font and acceptable for resumes. Using it will keep you from having to make a lot of format and style changes on your resume.

An online search for "resume fonts" will give you other alternatives. The following is a sample list of acceptable fonts:

- Arial
- Book Antiqua
- Calibri
- Cambria
- Didot
- Garamond
- Georgia
- Helvetica
- Times New Roman
- Trebuchet MS
- Verdana

*Font Size*

Acceptable font size can vary depending on the font you use and your space management needs. But keep your normal font size between 10 and 12 points. You may use larger font sizes for names, titles, section headers, and so on. Just make sure you do not decrease your resume's readability by using fonts that are too small, too large, or disproportionate in size.

*Text Formatting*

Appropriate use of bold, italicized, or underlined text can help guide your readers through your resume and focus them on important information.

Make sure you use text formatting consistently and do not overuse it. Inconsistent use or overuse of text formatting can make your resume difficult to read.

*White Space*

To maximize readability and visual appeal, you should have appropriate white space on your resume. You should maintain reasonable margins on your resume and have appropriate spacing in your content and between resume sections.

Start with ¾ or one-inch margins on all sides of your resume. If you need page space, you can decrease the top and bottom margin size. I do not recommend going below half-inch margins on the top and bottom. Don't change the left or right margins. It is better to add a page than to try to cram everything into a limited space.

*Resume Length*

There are many opinions on how long a resume should be. Fundamentally, your resume should be ***as long as it needs to be*** to effectively, but concisely, communicate your fitness for your target job.

As a rule of thumb, if you have less than five to seven years of experience, a one-page resume should be sufficient. A two-page resume is appropriate for someone with over five to seven years of experience. If you are including over fifteen years of experience or have had a number of jobs, you might need a three-page resume.

I recommend trying to keep your resume to no more than two pages. If you haven't captured the interest of your reader in the first page or two, you are unlikely to do so with extra pages.

Still, don't get too stressed about resume length. Keep it focused and concise but make sure it contains the information necessary to demonstrate you are the right person for your target job.

*Multipage Resume Headers*

If your resume has more than one page, you will want to include a small header, starting on your second page.

Your header should include your name and the page number. You should be able to use your word processing header function to do this.

Just make sure you do not include a header on your first page and make sure your header has an appropriately sized font. You want the header to be noticeable but not distracting from the main body of the resume.

# Exercise #6
# Build Your Baseline Resume

At this point, building your baseline resume should be straightforward. You have already captured most of the information you need for your resume. It's just a matter of putting it all together.

Throughout this exercise, I provide examples of the different sections. I also provide examples of completed resumes at the end of this **Step**.

> *Winning Resume Tip*
>
> Everyone has different skills and experience, and it's impossible to give resume guidance for every possible circumstance. This exercise will cover the basics you need for your resume, but don't be afraid to add or modify if it's appropriate for your situation. Just remember to use your judgment and make sure that your final baseline resume meets the criteria for a winning resume and is *focused, concise, easy to read, error-free,* and *truthful.*

## *Exercise Step 1: Name and Contact Information*

At the top of your resume, type your name, center it, and use a larger font. You want your reader to see your name immediately. I recommend a 16- or 18-point font but see what works best for you. You can always adjust fonts once you have drafted your full resume.

Below your name should be your basic contact information including

- Phone number
- E-mail (make sure it's professional)
- City and state

Add your contact information centered on the next line, below your name, in the same order they are listed above. All the information can be on the same line. Separate each item with a vertical line bar (|). Usually, this character shares a key on your keyboard with the backslash (\). You can also use other symbols such as tildes (~), asterisks (*), or dashes (-) for separation. Use the font size you will use in the body of your resume (10 to 12 points).

## *Exercise Step 1: Example*

### Janet Becker

555-555-5555 | jbecker@example.com | Dallas, TX

---

### *Winning Resume Tip*

You should consider if it makes sense to include your LinkedIn profile address or other social media links (e.g., Twitter and Instagram) with your contact information. Only include your LinkedIn or other social media sites if they are professional, well-constructed, up to date, and consistent with the information on your resume.

Do not add any links to sites (e.g., Facebook) that include personal or potentially negative information you would not want a potential employer to see. You do not want to give an employer any reason not to hire you. When in doubt, do not add social media links.

If you do decide to add links, I recommend placing them between your email and your city/state on your contact information line. See the full resumes at the end of this **Step** for examples.

---

## *Exercise Step 2: Professional Summary*

Review the Professional Summary you developed in the previous **Step**. Make any final revisions.

Center and place your resume title below your contact information. Make sure there is at least one line between your contact information and your title. Use a slightly larger font. Make the title boldface, underline it, or create top and bottom border lines (see tip below), as appropriate.

Start your summary paragraph on the second line below your title. Use your normal font and font size (10–12 pts.). You should be able to cut and paste the material you developed in **Step 4**.

Place your list of key skills below your summary paragraph. You can simply place them on several centered lines using a vertical line bar (|) or another appropriate symbol to separate the individual skills. You can also list your skills in a vertical bulleted list in two or more columns.

If you have decided to use a title for your key skills section, make sure it is centered with a slightly larger font. Make the title boldface, underline it, or create top and bottom border lines, as appropriate.

## *Exercise Step 2: Example*

**Consumer Finance Operations Executive**

Transformative executive who elevates and improves operations across organizations. Team builder known for increasing sales and profitability, developing staff, and strengthening compliance controls. Specialist in turning around low-performing territories and branches with extensive experience in the consumer banking, mortgage, and insurance industries.

Operations Management | P&L Budgeting | Consumer Sales
Performance Management | Branch Operations | Change Management
Team Development and Training | Strategic Planning
AML Compliance & Fraud Prevention | Project Management
Process Improvement

> ## *Winning Resume Tip*
>
> You can use formatting tools in your word processing program to create lines or boxes on your resume. Check your word processing program and see what it can do.
>
> If you are using MS Word, on the Home menu in the Paragraph section there are shading and border buttons you can use.
>
> For more options, go to the Design menu. In the section titled Page Background, there is a Page Borders button. It will call up a Borders and Shading menu box. Make sure you are working in the Borders menu, not the Page Border menu. The Borders menu will allow you to place lines or boxes around specific paragraphs. Avoid the Page Border menu as it will format your entire page, which you do not want to do.

## *Exercise Step 3: Professional Experience*

Center "Professional Experience" just below your key skills section. Use a slightly larger font, use boldface, underline it, or create top and bottom border lines. Make sure you have left a space between the skills section in your Professional Summary and the title.

Continue placing the summaries of each of your jobs, in chronological order, below the section title. Make sure you leave appropriate space between each job.

You should be able to cut and paste from the material you developed in **Step 4.**

Remember, for each job, you should place the name of the company, the city and state, and the dates you worked there on the first line. Your title should be on the second line. Your job description and achievement bullet points should be below that.

Make sure you have appropriate spacing between each of your jobs.

## *Exercise Step 3: Example*

### Professional Experience

**LONE STAR MORTGAGE COMPANY, Dallas, TX**　　　　　　9/2017-Present
**Director of Branch Operations**

Leads branch business operations for $8B retail mortgage company with 30+ offices across Texas and Oklahoma. Oversees financial, operational, and compliance performance for all offices. Supervises all branch managers and 5 operational staff.

- Achieved 23% growth in branch revenues over two years by opening 5 new branches in Oklahoma.

- Improved territory profitability by 12%, with no loss of mortgage volume, by closing and consolidating 3 underperforming branches in the Dallas area.

- Spearheaded 17% improvement in customer service levels through new staff training program developed in conjunction with HR and IT departments.

- Led the successful deployment of a new mortgage underwriting system, leading to an average 20% reduction in mortgage processing times across all branches.

> ## *Winning Resume Tip*
>
> If you have gaps in your employment history, you will want to think about how you cover that timeframe in your Professional Experience. If the gap is for a relatively short period (a few months), you may not need to do anything. Just list your positions chronologically as normal.
>
> If you have gaps longer than a few months, you should go back and review your Career Inventory. If you performed consulting, freelance, volunteer, or some other work during your gap period, consider using them as positions in your Professional Experience. Remember, however, your resume must be *truthful*, so do not put anything in your Professional Experience that you cannot support.
>
> In the end, it may be better to leave the gap uncovered in your Professional Experience if you cannot identify a reasonable way to address it. It will undoubtedly raise a flag for your reader, but employment gaps are not unusual. You just need to be prepared to discuss the issue appropriately if a potential employer asks you about it.

## *Exercise Step 4: Education*

The last main section is for your education and any formal training you may have completed.

Center "Education" just below your last job in Professional Experience. Use the same font you used for other section titles and bold, underline, or create top and bottom border lines. Make sure you leave a space between the two sections.

Begin listing your degrees, starting with your most advanced. Spell out the name of your degree on one line. Use normal font but make the degree title boldface.

After the degree name, place a comma and then list your major or course of study if applicable.

On the next line, place your school's name followed by the school's city and state.

Don't list the dates of your degree or your GPA. Don't list your high school diploma, unless that is the highest level of education you have completed.

Repeat for your remaining degrees.

There are several education variations you may need to consider:

*Active student in a degree program.* Your first entry should reflect your current program. On the first line of the entry, list your target degree and your field of study. Follow that with "anticipated" or "expected" in parentheses, and your estimated completion date.

On the next line, place your school's name followed by its city and state.

*Incomplete degree.* If you have not completed a degree and are not actively working on one, list your program of study, and either the amount of time you attended the school or the number of credits you earned.

Place your school's name and location on the next line, as usual.

*Certificates/nondegree training programs.* If you have earned a certificate of some sort, or completed formal, nondegree training programs, you should include them in your Education section. Make sure you include the name of the certificate or program, the awarding organization, and the city and state if applicable.

## *Exercise Step 4: Examples*

### Education

**Master of Science**, Project Management (expected 12/2018)
University of Dallas, Dallas, TX

**Master of Business Administration**, Information Technology
Ohio State University, Columbus, OH

**Bachelor of Arts,** Electrical Engineering
St. John's University, Minneapolis, MN

**Certificate in Computer Forensics**
Collin County Community College, Frisco, TX

---

### Winning Resume Tip

To help maximize space or improve your resume's visual appeal, you can adjust the formatting of your Education section if necessary. Options include using abbreviations for your degrees (e.g., BA, MBA, Ph.D.) or placing your degree/certificate information all on one line.

---

## Exercise Step 5: Supplemental Sections

Depending on your background, you may want to include one or more supplemental sections to your baseline resume.

You should only include a supplemental section if it helps demonstrate your suitability for your target job.

Some sections could include the following:

- *Certifications and Licenses.* This section would be a list of any professional certifications or licenses you hold.

- *Professional Development.* If you have training or coursework that is not part of your Education section, you may list it in a professional development section.

- *IT Skills.* If you have not previously listed all your IT skills, you may want to create a supplemental section. It should be a list of IT skills, programming languages, major systems, and so on, with which you have experience and which are relevant to your target job.

- *Professional Associations.* List any professional association memberships you hold.

- *Volunteer Experience.* This section lists and summarizes your significant volunteer experience.

- *Military Experience.* If you are a veteran, you may want to list your military experience. Only use a separate section if your service was more than ten to fifteen years ago. Otherwise, you should place your military experience in your Professional Experience section. If you do include a separate Military Experience section, to avoid judgments about your age, you may not want to list your dates of service.

Based on your background, other potential supplemental sections may suggest themselves.

Use your judgment on how to format your supplemental sections. At this point in your resume, you want to keep them short and concise. Only provide just enough information to interest your resume reader.

Here are some examples:

## *Exercise Step 5: Examples*

### Certifications

Project Management Professional (PMP)
Agile Certified Professional (PMI-ACP)
Certified Scrum Professional (CSP)

### Military Experience

US ARMY
**Field Artillery Officer**
Positions held include Battalion Logistics Officer, Battery Executive Officer, and Assistant Battalion Operations

Finished with the exercise steps? Congratulations! You have drafted your baseline resume. Stop and take a break. If you can, wait a few hours, or even a day or two, before you move on to the next **Step**.

*Step 5 Checklist: Baseline Resume*

In **Step 5**, you should have:

- Reviewed recommendations on resume layouts and formatting
- Built your baseline resume including, at a minimum, your contact info, Professional Summary, Professional Experience, and Education sections

If you have missed anything, go back, review **Step 5** again, and complete any necessary items.

*Full Resume Samples*

The following are examples of completed resumes. There are some formatting differences between the resumes, but they all follow the basic structure outlined in this **Step**.

## Janet Becker
555-555-5555 | jbecker@example.com | Dallas, TX

### Consumer Finance Operations Executive

Transformative executive who elevates and improves operations across organizations. Team builder known for increasing sales and profitability, developing staff, and strengthening compliance controls. Specialist in turning around low-performing territories and branches with extensive experience in the consumer banking, mortgage, and insurance industries.

Operations Management | P&L Budgeting | Consumer Sales | Performance Management
Branch Operations | Conflict Management | Team Development and Training | Strategic Planning
AML Compliance & Fraud Prevention | Project Management | Change Management | Process Improvement

### Professional Experience

**LONE STAR MORTGAGE COMPANY**, Dallas, TX                                9/2017-Present
**Director of Branch Operations**
Leads branch business operations for $8B retail mortgage company with 30+ offices across Texas and Oklahoma. Oversees financial, operational, and compliance performance for all offices. Supervises all branch managers and 5 operational staff.
- Achieved 23% growth in branch revenues over two years by opening 5 new branches in Oklahoma.
- Improved territory profitability by 12%, with no loss of mortgage volume by closing and consolidating 3 underperforming branches in the Dallas area.
- Spearheaded 17% improvement in customer service levels through new staff training program developed in conjunction with HR and IT departments.
- Led the successful deployment of a new mortgage underwriting system, leading to an average 20% reduction in mortgage processing times across all branches.

**PCA NATIONAL BANK**, Dallas, TX                                             7/2008-8/2017
**Assistant Vice President – Consumer Banking**                                6/2014-8/2017
Managed regional retail sales and operations division encompassing 50+ branches across North Texas. Administered multimillion-dollar expense budget. Ensured proper functioning of day-to-day branch operations including vault duties, cash level management, over/short cash controls, and fraud prevention. Coordinated all Federal and internal audit activities in branches.
- Consistently exceeded territory profit, deposit growth, sales, and lending goals over two-year period.
- Reduced territory expenses by 18% through aggressive management of vendor expenses.
- Implemented new fraud control procedures across branches that stopped over $300,000 in theft, fraud, and cash mismanagement losses.
- Raised territory's average branch Federal Audit scores from 74% to 97% (out of 100%).

**Project Manager – Organizational Readiness**                                 2/2012-6/2014
Developed and directed change management and organizational readiness plan to transition 1,100 associates to new branch IT system.
- Coordinated successful rollout of new branch IT systems through 3-phase implementation over a 6-month period
- Led stakeholders and SMEs to update system policies and procedures to support BSA, Dodd-Frank, AML, Equal Credit Opportunity Act, Truth in Lending, Fair Credit Reporting Act and Credit Card Act compliance.

Janet Becker
Pg. 2

**PCA NATIONAL BANK** (cont.)
**District Manager**                                                                                                3/2010-2/2012
Promoted to turn-around 10 failing, high-risk branches in region. Supervised branch managers and monitored day-to-day branch operations. Coordinated Federal and internal audit activities in branches.
- Within a year, led district to exceed profit, deposit growth and sales goals through staff development, training, and various process improvement initiatives.
- Stopped annual losses of $200,000 through the implementation of new AML and anti-fraud controls.
- Reduced district operating and lease costs by 20% by rationalizing district geographic coverage and closing 2 branches.

**Branch Manager**                                                                                                  7/2008-2/2010
Managed all day-to-day operations, including customer service, cash control, vault procedures, and fraud prevention, for branch with $45M in deposits. Supervised and trained all sales and teller staff.
- Increased branch ranking from #1311 out of 1400 branches to #181 in less than one year.
- Requested by District Management to provide coaching to other branches to help improve operations across district branches.
- Received consistent Federal Audit scores of 97% (out of 100%).

**ARBOR LIFE INSURANCE COMPANY**                                                                                    9/2003-6/2008
**Quality Assurance Analyst**
Ensured company policies and procedures were compliant with applicable federal and state laws/regulations including HIPAA and federal/state labor laws.
- Developed and led staff training on HIPAA privacy regulations for 200+ associates leading to a 96% pass rate in staff testing.
- Implemented HIPAA compliance procedures and controls for company health services employee research program including Institutional Review Board (IRB) procedures and data privacy and security.

## Education

**Master of Science**, Project Management (Expected 12/2018)
University of Dallas, Dallas, TX

**Bachelor of Science**, Organizational Management
University of Texas, Arlington, TX

# John Mathews

555-555-5555 | jmathews@example.com | linkedin.com/in/profilename | Cincinnati, OH

## Senior IT Program and Project Manager

Dynamic program manager with track-record of delivering multimillion-dollar IT initiatives and projects that meet business requirements, on-time and on budget. Collaborative leader who builds high performing teams with business, technical and international staff. Certified Project Management and Agile Professional who introduces innovative project management techniques to improve project efficiency and effectiveness.

- Project Management Professional (PMP)
- Certified Scrum Professional (CSP)
- Agile Certified Professional (PMI-ACP)
- Software Development Lifecycle
- Budgeting and Forecasting
- Requirements Gathering and Analysis
- Offshore Development
- ERP Systems
- SaaS and Cloud Architecture
- Information Security
- User Training
- Quality Management

## Professional Experience

**ACME LIFE INSURANCE COMPANY, Cincinnati, OH**     2012–Present
**Senior IT Program Manager**
Leads enterprise system implementation programs for Fortune 500 Life Insurance Company with $43B in assets. Manages $25M program budget and 20+ project management staff. Oversees vendor relationships with key offshore development partners.

- Drove 22% improvement in customer satisfaction ratings through successful agile development and deployment of new customer account mobile app suite.
- Led $5M cloud migration of 110 applications and 500 system processes to cloud provider over 10-month period resulting in a 26% reduction in IT operational costs.
- Managed 2-year, $20M deployment of Oracle Financial Suite across all company subsidiaries. Completed program 3 months ahead of schedule and $2M under budget
- Achieved 28% savings on offshore development and staffing costs by consolidating number of offshoring partners from 8 to 3.

**MIDWEST NATIONAL BANK, Cincinnati, OH**     2008–2012
**Project Manager**
Recruited to develop project management best practices and lead major system deployments at regional bank with $20B in assets. Managed over 20 projects with 10-50 project staff and budgets between $1M and $10M.

- Led joint client/vendor project management team for deployment of new operating system across 300+ branches. Worked closely with vendor team to ensure project was on time and budget and system customizations met all business requirements.
- Turned-around struggling $3,000,000 data warehouse and business intelligence system project. Successfully reset expectations with business stakeholders, development staff, and executives and delivered project within revised schedule and budget.
- Reduced average software project delivery time by 17% by developing and presenting project best practices training to IT project management staff.

John Mathews
Page 2

**SUMMIT CONSULTING, Columbus, OH** 2000-2008
**Manager/Senior Consultant**
Consulted with financial services and manufacturing clients on system design, development, and implementation best practices as part of boutique consulting firm with 400 staff. Led and supported a range of process improvement and system implementation projects. Supervised consulting teams of 3-10 staff.

- As project manager, delivered, on-time and on-budget, $10M JD Edwards ERP implementation for security device manufacturer.
- Designed and managed organizational deployment and staff training plan for SAP ERP system at auto parts manufacturer leading to successful adoption of system by key business departments.
- Redesigned IT department change control policies for regional credit union leading to improved project budget and schedule management and a 20% reduction in project change requests across organization.
- Achieved a two-month reduction in the time required to develop business requirements for SAP ERP system implementation at an air-conditioner manufacturer.

## Education

**Master of Business Administration**, Information Technology
Ohio State University, Columbus, OH

**Bachelor of Arts,** Electrical Engineering
St. John's University, Minneapolis, MN

## Certifications

Project Management Professional (PMP)
Agile Certified Professional (PMI-ACP)
Certified Scrum Professional (CSP)

## Military Experience

US ARMY
**Field Artillery Officer**
Positions held include Battalion Logistics Officer, Battery Executive Officer, and Assistant Battalion Operations Officer.

# Michael Cortez

555-555-5555 | mcortez@example.com | Houston, TX

---

### LOGISTICS & DISTRIBUTION OPERATIONS MANAGER

---

- Proactive operations manager who continually looks for opportunities to improve processes, reduce costs, and maximize operational efficiency.
- Collaborative supervisor who builds high-performing teams by connecting with staff, promoting operational goals, and training team members on new processes and procedures.

Logistics | Warehouse Operations | Shipping & Receiving | Distribution | Process Improvement
Team-Building & Leadership | Customer Service | Safety | Quality Control

---

### PROFESSIONAL EXPERIENCE

---

CORINTH TILE, Houston, TX                                    2015-Present
**Operations Supervisor**                                    2017-Present

Oversees operations at 700,000 sq. ft. distribution center, including inbound, outbound, less-than-truckload (LTL), and small package (SPC) logistics. Supervises 30 team members, facility quality control, and safety procedures on assigned shift.

- Co-led design and implementation of new shift schedule, moving facility from two to four shifts, resulting in 99.96% on-time shipping and approx. 10% reduction in labor costs.
- Achieved 99.95% correct/undamaged (ITD) shipping rate by identifying and introducing new packing materials and boxes and shifting to new material vendor.
- Co-led development of SOPs for distribution center operations that were implemented across three primary company facilities.
- Key contributor to implementation of first-ever labor management system that reduced staff administration time and helped reduce labor costs.

**Shift Lead**                                                2015-2017

Managed all aspect of day-to-day operations for assigned stations, including Inbound, Outbound, and LTL. Supervised receiving, outbound shipments, vehicle loading/loading, logistics administration, warehouse storage, and general dock management.

- Restructured inbound dock operations, reducing the number of receiving docks required for operations by 50% (four to two docks).
- Worked with management team to redesign LTL handling procedures, resulting in significant improvements in on-time shipping rates and number of correct/undamaged shipments.
- Implemented new control procedures that reduced the number of lost shipping documents and enabled team to clear major backlog of freight on docks.

GREEN-GROW FERTILIZER, Houston, TX                           2014-2015
**Merchandiser**

Managed in-store displays and stock at multiple retail locations across four-city territory. Led customer and sales events at selected retail locations in support of company marketing campaigns.

- Selected to assist and travel with Regional Manager across sales region in support of annual merchandising replacement.

---

### EDUCATION

---

**Associate of Arts**, General Studies
Houston Community College, Houston, TX

# Step 6
## Check Your Resume

Now you are ready to check your baseline resume. Make sure you have taken a break and focused on something else for a bit. If you try to check your resume right after writing it, chances are you will miss something that needs to be corrected.

**Exercise #7**
**Check Your Resume**

To check your resume, I recommend several different steps. This exercise will walk you through them.

*Exercise Step 1: Use Your Automated Review Tools*

First, you should use your word processor's automated review functions. Your word processor is probably already set up to highlight grammar and spelling errors when you are writing a document.

If you haven't already corrected highlighted errors, go through your resume, and correct them now.

Once you have corrected any visible errors, you should manually trigger a full spelling and grammar review by your word processor. A full review may uncover errors or issues your word processor did not highlight when you were building your resume.

> ## Winning Resume Tip
>
> Consider using other proofreading applications to check your resume. Proofreading applications are more advanced and can identify grammatical issues better than your word processor. The downside is proofreading applications may not be free. You may not want to spend the extra money just to check your resume. But if you do a lot of writing, even if it is just e-mail, you might find the investment worth it.
>
> I recommend grammarly.com, but there are other options. Perform an online search for "proofreading applications" to find alternatives.

## Exercise Step 2: Check for Format and Punctuation Consistency

Next, check your resume for format and punctuation consistency. Make sure you are consistent throughout the resume. Things you want to look at include the following:

- Fonts
- Spacing
- Punctuation (e.g., use of periods at the end of bullet points that are complete sentences)

Checking for consistency is an important step in your review. Your resume will leave a bad impression with a reader if it has formatting or punctuation inconsistencies.

I recommend you review a printed copy of your resume as well as reviewing it on your screen. You are likely to notice different issues in a printed version from those you view on a screen. A reviewer may look at your resume electronically, or in hard copy, so you want to make sure you check both.

## *Exercise Step 3: Read Your Resume Aloud*

It may sound silly, but the best way to manually check your resume is to read it aloud. Many people fail to notice issues because they just visually scan their resume. They do not take the time to review it properly.

Reading your resume aloud forces you to review it slowly. It is a great way to catch both style and grammatical errors.

Reading it aloud also lets you check how your resume sounds. If it doesn't sound right to you, it won't look right to a reader.

As you read your resume, ask yourself the following questions:

*Is my resume focused?* Does it strongly position me for my target job? Does it communicate my unique value and the results I have delivered to employers?

*Is my resume concise?* Does it provide just enough information to interest reviewers and make them want to interview me or take the next step in the hiring process?

*Is my resume easy to read?* Does its formatting make it easy for reviewers to scan and find the information they need?

*Is my resume error-free?* Is it free of any content, format, or punctuation mistakes or inconsistencies?

*Is my resume truthful?* Does it only contain information that I can back up in an interview or during a background check?

If the answers to the above questions are yes, you are in good shape. If the answer is no to any of them, you need to make changes.

Make corrections as you go, or note issues and correct them later. Once you've made your revisions, read your resume aloud again. You want to make sure your revisions are error-free as well.

## Exercise Step 4: Check for Visual Appeal

The first judgment any reviewer will make is whether your resume is visually appealing. A visually unappealing resume will immediately put you at a disadvantage.

Once you have completed all your revisions, take a final look at your resume, both on the screen and in print. Ask yourself if your resume looks good. If you are not convinced it does, you need to go back and make changes to your layout and formatting.

---

### Winning Resume Tip

Make sure you check the page breaks in your resume. Poorly placed page breaks can disrupt the flow of your resume and create confusion for the reader.

If you have a problematic page break, try adjusting your spacing, margins, or even font size. It might be better to have a little additional white space on one page to avoid breaking up parts of a key section or entry. With any changes you make, use your judgment on what will look and flow the best for the reader.

---

## Exercise Step 5: Have Someone Else Read Your Resume

The final check you should complete is having someone else review your resume. Give it to a family member, friend, or several different people, and ask them to critique it.

Ask your reviewer(s) to answer some of the same questions you asked yourself:

- Does the resume look good?
- Is the resume focused, concise, easy to read, and error-free?

Take note of their recommendations and consider what you should change. Correct any formatting, grammatical, or punctuation errors. Make any content or style changes that strengthen your resume.

> *Winning Resume Tip*
>
> Make sure you use a professional file name when you save your resume. I recommend including your name in the title, in some fashion, so a reader can easily identify it. For customized resumes (see next step), you can also include information related to the target job or company.

Finished with all your corrections and revisions? If you are, great job! You have fully completed your baseline resume. As mentioned in **Step 5**, you can use your baseline resume for several purposes. You can

- Post it to an online job board
- Send it to recruiters
- Share it with networking contacts
- Customize it to apply for specific jobs

The final **Step** addresses how to customize your baseline resume for specific jobs.

## Step 6 Checklist: Resume Check

In **Step 6**, you should have

- Used automated review tools to check your resume
- Checked for formatting and punctuation consistency
- Read your resume aloud and made any necessary changes
- Checked your resume for visual appeal
- Had someone else review your resume and made any necessary changes

If you have missed anything, go back, review **Step 6** again, and complete any necessary items.

# Step 7
## Customize Your Baseline Resume

Whenever you apply for a specific job, you should customize your baseline resume.

Even if the new job is like your general target job, it will still have unique requirements. To create a winning resume and maximize your chances of getting an interview, you must align your resume with those requirements.

Fortunately, you should be in good shape. You can use your baseline resume and Career Inventory together to create a customized resume that matches you to the new job.

## Exercise #8
## Customize Your Baseline Resume

In this exercise, you will review a specific job description and revise your baseline resume to better match you to the job.

## Exercise Step 1: Review the Job Description and Identify Requirements and Keywords

Review the job description and identify the specific keywords and core requirements. Requirements can include

- Responsibilities
- Skills (both hard and soft)
- Experience
- Level of education
- Certifications or licenses

If you are having a hard time identifying keywords, don't forget you can use online tools such as a word cloud generator (www.wordclouds.com or www.wordle.net).

## Exercise Step 2: Compare to Your Target Job Requirements and Keywords

Compare the requirements and keywords you identified from your specific job description with your target job requirements and keywords from **Step 3**.

Note any requirements or keywords that are unique to the new job.

## Exercise Step 3: Revise Your Baseline Resume

Based on the new job's specific keywords or unique requirements, begin revising your baseline resume. Review each of the following resume sections along with your Career Inventory. Make changes, as necessary, to better align your resume with the new job description.

*Professional Summary*

*Professional title.* Consider revising your resume title to align with the new job description. Doing so can immediately cause the reader to associate you with the job description.

*Summary paragraph.* Look at your Professional Summary. Make any adjustments you think would strengthen it for the new job. Look for ways to include keywords from the new job description.

*Skills list.* Review your list of skills. Consider updating the list to include skills you might have that are unique to the new job description. Remove any skills from your current list that may be unnecessary.

*Professional Experience*

*Job titles.* Look at your job titles and determine if it's appropriate to update any of them to better align with the new job description.

*Job descriptions.* Review your descriptions of previous jobs and your Career Inventory. Consider adjusting your descriptions so they correlate with the new job requirements. Try to include any new keywords or phrases naturally.

*Results/achievements.* Examine each of the results/achievements bullet points for your previous jobs. Consider replacing or updating bullet points that do not strongly match the new job's requirements. Select other results/achievements, if any, from your Career Inventory that are a better fit.

**Remember, only make revisions that you can back up with your experience.** Refer to your Career Inventory to identify additional skills and experiences you can use to support your changes.

It is unlikely that you will need to customize your other resume sections, such as Education. Still, it is worth doing a quick check to see if you can strengthen any other part of your resume.

## Exercise Step 4: Check Your Customized Resume

Since you have changed your baseline resume, you must check the new version for issues or errors. You should follow most of the basic steps that we outlined in **Step 6** including the following:

- Use automated review tools.
- Check format and punctuation consistency.

- Read your resume aloud.
- Check for visual appeal.

It's probably impractical to have someone else review every customized resume you create, but it may be worth doing for important job applications.

Once you have checked and revised your customized resume, you are ready to use it.

Make sure that you save your customized resume under a different name from that of your baseline resume. You will want to be able to track which resume you submitted for any given opportunity.

> ### Winning Resume Tip
>
> Be aware of how much time you spend customizing resumes. Customizing your resume does not mean you should spend hours trying to wordsmith every section. In many cases, your baseline resume should be strong enough to submit with minimal adjustments.
>
> Remember, the more time you spend customizing resumes, the less time you are looking for additional job opportunities. Use your judgment on where your job search time is best spent.

Congratulations! You have completed the *7 Steps to a Winning Resume*.

You should now have a resume that demonstrates, better than other candidates' resumes, how you can deliver results for a future employer. Your resume should significantly increase your chances of getting interviews and having a successful job search.

Just as important, you now have the information, tools, and process you need to customize your resume and show how your skills and experiences match the requirements for specific positions.

The next section covers alternative resume formats appropriate for career changers, people returning to the workforce, or new graduates. If you are not in any of those categories, then skip to the last section where we share some final tips.

> *Step 7 Checklist: Customized Resumes*
>
> In **Step 7**, you should have
>
> - Identified unique job requirements and keywords for the specific job you are applying for
> - Revised your baseline resume to create a customized resume aligned with the specific job
> - Checked your customized resume for issues or errors
>
> If you have missed anything, go back, review **Step 7** again, and complete any necessary items.

# Alternative Resume Formats

If you are switching careers, returning to the workforce, or a new graduate, you may benefit from using a different resume format. In the next two exercises, we will cover how to build effective resumes more suited to your needs.

**Exercise #9**
**Build a Hybrid Resume**

If you are trying to switch careers or returning to the workforce, then a hybrid resume that combines elements of both the functional and chronological resume formats may be helpful. A hybrid resume will have an expanded Professional Summary to best show how your experience and skills make you a fit for your target job, regardless of where, or how long ago, you got them.

Let's walk through the steps you need to follow to make a hybrid resume. Several of these steps will point you back to exercises described earlier in this guide.

## Exercise Step 1: Complete Your Career Inventory

Start by creating a Career Inventory as outlined in *Exercise #1* in **Step 1**.

If you have not been working for a while, expand your Career Inventory by creating a section that highlights all the activities or projects you completed while out of the workforce. You'd be surprised at how many transferable skills you can identify from the day-to-day tasks required to manage your life and family.

Also, make sure that you identify and document any volunteer experience you have.

## Exercise Step 2: Identify Your PVP

Next, identify your PVP as outlined in *Exercise #2* in **Step 2**.

## Exercise Step 3: Define Your Target Job

Continue by defining your target job, as outlined in *Exercise #3* in **Step 3**.

## Exercise Step 4: Create Your Professional Summary

Creating your Professional Summary is where the resume building process begins to change from the standard **Steps**. In a hybrid resume, you will have three main Professional Summary components including the following:

- Professional title
- Summary paragraph(s)
- Selected results and achievements (bullet points)

Let's walk through how to create each of them.

*Professional Title*

Your professional title is a concise description of the type of job you want. You should base it on your target job, but it should also reflect your experience. Your resume title can either be very specific or more general, depending on your preference.

Take a few minutes and draft a few versions. Pick the one that you think best represents your target job and your experience.

*Summary Paragraph*

Review the PVP you created in **Exercise Step 2**. Write one or two summary paragraphs that describe your unique value, your experience, and how you meet the requirements for your target job.

Use the PVP statements you created to help make your paragraph(s) as impactful as possible. Review your target job and make sure your summary paragraph reflects its requirements and includes appropriate keywords.

*Selected Results and Achievements*

Review all the results and achievements you identified in your Career Inventory. Select three to six that best relate to your target job's requirements. Create bullet point summaries for each one.

Your bullet points should include at least two core elements:

- The specific result you achieved or value you provided
- The actions you took to achieve the result

To strengthen the bullet points, you can also include contextual information on the challenge or situation you faced when delivering the result.

When writing the bullet points, place the core elements in whatever order makes sense. Whenever possible, you should start your bullet points with the results you achieved.

You should also review your target job keywords and phrases and include them in your bullet points if possible.

You will place your list of results and achievements directly below your summary paragraph.

You may also opt to create a separate section. If you do, there are different section titles you can use including the following:

- Selected Achievements
- Professional Highlights
- Major/Key Accomplishments

Or you can use some other appropriate title.

## *Exercise Step 5: Create Your Key Skill Section*

Another difference between a hybrid resume and a chronological resume is the inclusion of a separate skills section. There are two parts to this section: a skill list, and a set of key skill examples.

Let's look at the instructions for each.

### *Skills List*

Review your Career Inventory and pick nine to fifteen of your key skills. Make sure you select skills that are relevant to your target job. Your skills list is also a good place to include appropriate keywords and phrases.

### *Key Skills Examples*

Review your target job and select three to five of the most important skills required for the job. For each of these skills, write a brief description of how you have previously demonstrated this skill. Use your Career Inventory to help you write the descriptions. Some examples are below.

**Consultative Selling** - Grew major account revenues over 137% through consultative selling of service solutions across client organization.

**Account Management** - Helped rescue region's largest account by providing superior customer support and addressing numerous outstanding customer service issues promptly.

**Prospecting** - Built $700,000 annual book of business from scratch for medical practice accounts receivable company.

**Sales Management** - Improved restaurant services company's regional sales team ranking to #17 from #84 (out of 123 regions).

**Marketing Collateral** - Worked with national marketing team to develop and test advertising and marketing collateral for new line of commercial refrigeration units.

When you place this skills section in your resume, you will want to have an appropriate title. Some options include the following:

- Key Skills
- Core Competencies
- Core Skills
- Skills Summary

Or some other title that is appropriate for your skill set and target job.

## *Exercise Step 6: Draft Your Professional Experience*

To draft your Professional Experience, you should follow *Exercise #4* in **Step 4** with two adjustments.

When you draft bullet point summaries of your results and achievements for each of your positions you should

- Provide at least two to three bullet points per position (more if you can)
- Make sure you do not repeat results/achievement bullets you used in your Professional Summary

Other than these changes, you should be able to follow the exercise as originally outlined.

## Exercise Step 7: Build Your Baseline Hybrid Resume

Now you are ready to build your baseline resume. You can follow the basic guidelines outlined in *Exercise #6* in **Step 5**. The only difference is you will have some extra components and sections. Your resume sections should be in the following order:

- Name and contact information
- Professional Summary
    - Professional title
    - Summary paragraph
    - Selected results and achievements
- Key Skills
    - Skills list
    - Key skills examples
- Professional Experience
- Education
- Other sections as appropriate

When you place your Professional Summary in your resume, you may opt to make a separate section for your selected results and achievements. Just make sure you have an appropriate section title (see the resume examples below).

## Exercise Step 8: Check Your Resume

Last, but not least, check your resume. You can follow the instructions in *Exercise #7*, found in **Step 6**.

## Exercise Step 9: Customize Your Resume

As you do with any other resume, you should customize a hybrid resume whenever you apply for a specific job. You can follow *Exercise #8* from **Step 7** to customize your resume. Updating your Professional Summary and key skills sections should be the primary focus of your customization.

Don't forget to recheck your resume once you have made changes.

The following are examples of a hybrid resume.

---

## Kimberly Post
555-555-5555 | kpost@example.com | Flower Mound, TX

### Experienced Account Manager

Multi-award winning, growth-focused sales professional with experience in account management and outside sales. Top producer proficient in consultative selling that goes above and beyond to satisfy customers, build strong relationships and close the sale. Business to business (B2B) sales expert in restaurant and hospitality markets with track record of increasing territory revenues. Key achievements include:

- Top regional sale representative for commercial food-service equipment distributor 3 years running, exceeding sales quotas by over 125% each year.
- Leveraged consultative selling skills to close $21M equipment sale, largest in company history, to national hotel chain.
- Increased regional revenues by 22% for restaurant services company by reorganizing sales territory and shifting focus to selling multi-service packages to key accounts.
- Grew sales territory by 52% by signing over 120 new clients over 1-year period.

### Core Competencies

| | | |
|---|---|---|
| • Consultative Selling | • Marketing Collateral | • Sales Management |
| • Account Management | • Lead Qualification | • Customer Service |
| • Contract Negotiation | • B2B Sales | • Inside Sales |
| • Prospecting | • Outside Sales | • Sales Presentations |

**Consultative Selling** – Grew major account revenues over 137% through consultative selling of service solutions across client organization.
**Account Management** – Helped rescue region's largest account by providing superior customer support and addressing numerous outstanding customer service issues promptly.
**Prospecting** – Built $700,000 annual book of business from scratch for medical practice accounts receivable company.
**Sales Management** – Improved restaurant services company's regional sales team ranking to #17 from #84 (out of 123 regions).
**Marketing Collateral** – Worked with national marketing team to develop and test advertising and marketing collateral for new line of commercial refrigeration units.

### Experience

RELIABLE DISTRIBUTORS, Irving, TX                              2009-2013
**Account Manager**
Managed regional and national sales accounts and outside sales for restaurant equipment distributor. Led business development, lead qualification, contract negotiations and customer issue resolution. Client base included restaurants, hotels, school districts, colleges and other hospitality organizations.

- Drove 50% growth in national accounts by spearheading effort to target restaurant and hotel chains headquartered in region through strategic account planning, the development of tailored marketing collateral, and enhanced sales presentations.
- Helped develop "green" sales strategy for new energy-efficient, environmentally friendly commercial oven equipment, resulting in initial sales exceeding targets by 32%.

Kimberly Post
Pg. 2

US SERVICES, Dallas, TX                                                                                                 2004-2009
**Sales Manager**                                                                                                       2007-2009
Promoted to lead team of 4 outside sales representatives to cover Dallas/Ft. Worth territory for national restaurant services company. Oversaw all major accounts and developed overall account strategy for territory.
- Helped increase territory closing rate by working with inside sales department to streamline the hand-off process for qualified prospects.
- Developed and led sales training exercises for territory, leading to a 30% increase in sales representative productivity.

**Outside Sales Representative**                                                                                        2004-2007
Prospected new customers, followed-up on leads generated by internal sales, and covered 40+ existing customer accounts.
- Top 10 regional sales representative for 2005 (#8) & 2006 (#6), consistently beating annual sales quotas.
- Led local territory in prospecting new clients, closing over 80 contracts over 3-year period.

MED-ACCOUNT, Plano, TX                                                                                                  2002-2004
**Sales Representative**
Developed local book of business for national medical practice account receivable processing company. Conducted market research, phone sales, and sales canvassing in support of business development.
- Achieved the fastest book-of-business growth in territory over 18-month period.
- Awarded 2013 gold-level national sales award.

## Education

**Bachelor of Arts**, Communications                                                                                    2002
University of Texas, Austin, TX

---

**Daniel Wilson**

555-555-5555 | dwilson@example.com | linkedin.com/in/profilename | Cupertino, CA

---

**Software Project Manager & Programmer**

Innovative software project manager with experience working with agile development methodologies. Driven profession who uses his hands-on programming experience to build integrated project and technical teams that exceed stakeholder expectations. Multi-year experience in mobile application development. Key achievements include:

- Project managed development of bestselling productivity app, TaskIt, voted top-10 new app for 2017 by *Mobile* (trade magazine).
- Reduced app development cycle time by 26% by introducing advanced scrum methodologies to project teams.
- Reduced development time by one month, for troubled, behind schedule, hotel reservation mobile app, after taking over as project manager, ensuring project was delivered on time and met stakeholder expectations.

---

**Key Skills**

---

- Project Management
- Agile Development
- Software Development

- Mobile Applications
- Business Analysis
- iOS/Android

- Python/Java/Ruby
- My SQL/PHP/HTML
- Quality Assurance

**Project Management** – Managed development and delivery of multiple mobile applications from project inception through go-live.
**Agile Development** – Utilized agile development/scrum methodologies on 30+ app development projects.
**Business Analysis** – Worked with customer focus groups, clients, and UI engineers on multiple projects to understand and document customer requirements and expectations for applications.

---

**Experience**

---

M FACTORY, Santa Clara, CA                                                                                                  2014-Present
**Project Manager/Sr. Mobile Developer**
Promoted to act as project manager for multiple projects at mobile application development firm. Uses agile methodologies to manage project schedules, staffing plans, and project budgets. Acts as senior software developer on selected projects.

- Assumed management of 4 mobile app development projects mid-stream after unexpected departure of previous project manager. Worked collaboratively with project teams to minimize disruptions, resulting in all projects being delivered on time and budget.
- Lead architect of GetFit! Android application (phone, tablet, and watch) developed for national fitness center company.

HJ Hotels, Plano, TX                                                                                                                2010-2014
**Software Programmer**
Mobile software developer for national hotel chain. Supported multiple aspects of app development including design, architecture, programming, and quality control.

- Helped increase housekeeping productivity by 17% across chain as part of team that architected and developed innovative room cleaning scheduling application.
- Led design and architecture of new maintenance request tracking application utilized in all company-owned hotels and several major franchises.

---

**Education**

---

**Bachelor of Arts**, Computer Science
Oklahoma State University, Stillwater, OK

---

# Exercise #10
# Building a New Graduate Resume

---

As a new graduate, you have unique challenges when writing a resume - the biggest being you likely have limited experience. Your resume will need to highlight your education and the skills you developed in school or in whatever jobs you may have had.

The next exercise will take you through the steps required to write a new graduate resume. Several of these steps will reference exercises described earlier in the book.

## *Exercise Step 1: Complete Your Career Inventory*

Start by creating a Career Inventory as outlined in *Exercise #1* in **Step 1**.

Expand your Career Inventory by including a section to cover your time in school. Make sure you include things such as

- Completed projects (particularly if relevant for your target job)
- Key skills developed through coursework
- GPA
- Academic honors
- Volunteer activities
- Clubs and activities
- School leadership positions
- IT skills or systems
- Names of advisors
- Names of key teachers
- Any other information you think relevant

You may not use all this information on your resume, but you may find much of it useful as you go through your job search.

## *Exercise Step 2: Identify Your PVP*

Next, identify your PVP as outlined in *Exercise #2* in **Step 2**.

You may find writing your PVP difficult if you have limited experience. Try focusing on the skills and personal attributes that made you successful at school. Many of these will carry over into your professional career. You can also focus on the skills you developed in your area of study (academic major, etc.), from your academic work, and from projects you have completed.

## *Exercise Step 3: Define Your Target Job*

Continue by defining your target job, as outlined in *Exercise #3* in **Step 3.**

## *Exercise Step 4: Draft Your Professional Summary*

As with a hybrid resume, creating your Professional Summary is where the resume building process changes from the guide's standard steps. The main difference is the new graduate resume will only have two parts:

- Your professional title
- A summary paragraph(s)

You will place your key skills in a separate section.

Let's walk through each part of your Professional Summary.

### *Professional Title*

Your professional title is a concise description of the type of job you want. You should base it on your target job, but it should also reflect your experience. Your resume title can either be very specific or more general depending on your preference.

Take a few minutes to draft a few versions. Pick the one you think best represents your target job and your level of experience.

### *Summary Paragraph*

Review the PVP you created in **Exercise Step 2.** Write a summary paragraph that describes your unique value and experience and how you meet the requirements for your target job.

Use the PVP statements you created to help make your paragraph as impactful as possible. Review your target job and make sure your summary reflects the job's requirements and includes appropriate keywords.

## Exercise Step 5: Create Your Key Skills Section

As mentioned in the previous exercise step, you will create a separate key skills section. There are two parts to this section: a skills list, and a set of key skills examples.

Let's look at the instructions for each.

### Skills List

Review your Career Inventory and pick nine to fifteen of your key skills. Make sure you select skills that are relevant to your target job. Your skills list is also a good place to include appropriate keywords and phrases.

### Key Skills Examples

Review your target job and select three to five of the most important skills required for the job. For each of these skills write a brief description of how you have previously demonstrated this skill. Use your Career Inventory to help you write the descriptions. Some examples are below.

**Budgeting** - Consolidated $20M of departmental budgets for inclusion into corporate budget for regional construction company.

**Accounts payable/receivable** - Conducted mid-year control audits of accounts payable/receivable department at $6B consumer goods company.

**Financial analysis** - Member of student team that conducted customer purchasing financial analysis for regional flooring distributor.

**Financial statements** - Assisted staff accountant in the preparation of annual financial statements for local child-services nonprofit organization.

When you place your separate skills section in your resume, you will want to have an appropriate title. Some options include

- Key Skills
- Core Competencies
- Core Skills
- Skills Summary

Or some other title that is appropriate for your skill set and target job.

## *Exercise Step 6: Draft Your Professional Experience Section*

To draft your Professional Experience section, you should follow *Exercise #4* in **Step 4** with one change.

When you draft bullet point summaries of your results and achievements for each of your positions, you should limit yourself to two to three bullet points per position. You may also decide not to include any bullet points at all if you do not have any strong results/achievements, or if you have already used examples to highlight your key skills.

## *Exercise Step 7: Draft Your Education Section*

Begin listing your degrees, starting with your most advanced.

Spell out the name of your degree on one line. Use normal font but bold the degree title. After your degree title, list your field of study or major. You can also include a minor if you have one.

For this type of resume, you should align your graduation year with the right margin of the same line.

On the next line place your school's name followed by the school's city and state.

If you have a GPA equal to, or better than, 3.5, then list your GPA as well. You can also list honors if you have graduated *cum laude, magna cum laude, summa cum laude,* and so on, or if you have other academic awards.

Repeat for any other degrees.

Don't list your high school diploma.

## *Exercise Step 8: Build Your Baseline Resume*

Now you are ready to build your baseline resume. You can follow the basic guidelines outlined in *Exercise #6* in **Step 5**. The only difference is you will have some different sections and a different order. Your resume sections should be in the following order:

- Name and contact information
- Professional Summary
  - Professional title
  - Summary paragraph
- Key skills
  - Skills list
  - Key skills examples
- Education
- Professional Experience
- Other sections as appropriate (e.g., academic achievements/awards, volunteer, and leadership experience)

When you place the different sections in your resume, make sure you have appropriate titles for each of them. (See the full resume example below)

As a new graduate, your resume only needs to be one page, so don't try to beef up your resume with information not relevant to your target job. An exception is if you have had significant work experience before earning your degree. In that case, use your judgment.

## Exercise Step 9: Check Your Resume

Make sure you check your resume. You can follow the instructions in *Exercise #7*, found in **Step 6**.

## Exercise Step 10: Customize Your Resume

You should always try to customize your resume when you apply for a specific job. You can follow *Exercise #8* from **Step 7** to customize your resume. Updating your Professional Summary and key skills sections should be the primary focus of your customization.

Don't forget to check your resume one last time before you send it out.

The resume below is an example of a new graduate resume.

# Jonathan Webber

555-555-5555 | jwebber@example.com | Raleigh, NC

## Finance and Accounting Associate

New finance and accounting professional with corporate, non-profit, and accounting firm exposure. Practical experience in departmental budgeting, financial analysis, and accounts payable/receivable. Detailed oriented worker with exceptional customer service and team-building skills.

## Key Skills

- Financial Analysis & Budgeting
- Corporate Accounting
- Accounts Payable/Receivable
- Account Reconciliation
- Customer Service
- Accounting Systems
- Financial Statements
- QuickBooks
- Bookkeeping

**Budgeting** – Consolidated $20M of departmental budgets for inclusion into corporate budget for regional construction company.
**Accounts Payable/Receivable** – Conducted mid-year control audits of Accounts Payable/Receivable department at $6B consumer goods company.
**Financial Analysis** – Member of student team that conducted customer purchasing financial analysis for regional flooring distributor.
**Financial Statements** – Assisted staff accountant in the preparation of annual financial statements for local child-services non-profit organization.

## Education

**Bachelor of Science,** Accounting & Finance                                   2017
North Carolina State University, Raleigh, NC                                    3.7 GPA
*Member – Beta Alpha Psi (Accounting Honor Society)*

## Experience

BEACON HOUSE, Raleigh, NC                                                        9/2016-5/2017
**Assistant Bookkeeper**
Supported all accounting operations for local child-care and after-school program non-profit with annual budget of $3 million.

BIG 4 ACCOUNTING FIRM, Raleigh, NC                                               5/2016-8/2016
**Accounting Intern**
Assisted with financial statement and control audits at $6B consumer goods company.

BAKER CONSTRUCTION, Raleigh, NC                                                  6/2015-9/2015
**Finance Intern**
Worked for Corporate Finance and Budgeting group at regional, diversified construction company.

MARIO'S PIZZA, Cary, NC                                                          Summer 2013 & 2014
**Shift Leader**
Evening shift leader for popular local pizza restaurant. Oversaw 6 wait staff and evening closing procedures.

# Some Final Winning Resume Tips

Just because you have written your resume doesn't mean it's the end of your work. As you go through your job search and career, you will need to make updates and changes to your resume. Here are some additional tips to help you out.

## *Improving Your Baseline Resume*

No resume is perfect, and your baseline resume should not be a static document during your job search. Ask readers for feedback on your resume. See how well it sells you to employers and gets you interviews.

Take time to evaluate the feedback and results. Identify ways you can strengthen your baseline resume and make changes. The more you can improve your resume and meet employer expectations, the more likely you are to have a successful job search.

## Additional Baseline Resumes

When looking for a new job, you may not want to limit yourself to one target job. You may have held different types of positions over your career and may be interested in more than one type of opportunity.

If this is the case, you should create a baseline resume for each of the target jobs that are significantly different from each other. If your target jobs are similar, you may be able to get by with customizing your original baseline resume, as described in **Step 7**.

To create additional baseline resumes, all you need to do is repeat **Steps 3** through **Step 6** for each new target job.

You should be able to use your Career Inventory and PVP from **Steps 1** and **2** since they are based on your work history, which doesn't change with different target jobs. Still, you may want to update your Career Inventory and PVP if you have additional information related to your new target job(s).

## PDF and ASCII Resumes

MS Word is the word processing program most businesses use today. Most online job boards and ATS systems can process Word documents. But there may be instances where you need to use a different file format such as PDF or ASCII (plain text).

### PDF Resumes

A PDF version of your resume can be useful when you are sending it to an individual. Many people now use mobile devices to look at documents. PDF files often display better and are easier to read on mobile devices than word processing documents.

A PDF resume can also help ensure your formatting does not become corrupted by different versions of word processing programs. This can be useful when you are sending it to someone you know will be printing it out.

But be careful submitting a PDF online to a company. Generally, ATS systems do not process PDF files well and may skip sections of your resume when scanning it for keywords.

There are several ways to convert your resume to a PDF. Most current versions of word processing programs, such as MS Word, allow you to save documents in a PDF format. Some programs also allow you to "print" to a PDF format as well. Alternatively, certain websites will convert a file to a PDF document for you. To find one, just do an online search for "PDF converter."

If you do use a PDF resume, make sure you open it in different viewers to verify that it looks okay. If there are problems with how it looks, go back and see if you need to adjust your original formatting.

*ASCII Resumes*

While unusual these days, you still may come across an online system that requires an ASCII format or requires you to cut and paste your resume. For this reason, you may need to create an ASCII resume.

The simplest way to make one is to use the "Save As" function in your word processing program and save your resume as a text file (.txt). You can also cut and paste your resume into a simple text editor such as Notepad.

Whichever method you use, you will need to update the text document formatting in your text editor or word processor. Some common issues you will see include the following:

- Text documents do not have tabs.
- There is no bolding, italicizing, or underlining of text.
- Bullets or other special symbols are not available; you can only use the characters present on your keyboard.
- The document only aligns with the left margin; you cannot center it or align it with the right margin.

Adjust the formatting of your text resume to make it as easy to read and as visually appealing as possible. Some formatting tips include the following:

- Place different pieces of personal information (e.g., name, phone number, email, city) on separate lines at the top of your resume.
- Replace bullets with other characters such as an asterisk (*), a plus sign (+), or a dash (-).
- Consider using lines of characters such as the equal sign (=) to separate resume sections.
- Consider using all capitals for resume section titles.

As always, use your judgment on what will work best for your resume. If it doesn't look right, fix it.

You can find more information and recommendations through an online search for "ASCII resumes."

## *Updating Your Career Inventory*

As we noted in a previous tip, you should periodically update your Career Inventory, even if you are not actively looking for a job. Consider updating your Career Inventory

- Every six to twelve months at your current job.
- When you change jobs.
- Whenever you have a major career event.

For your current job, you should focus on new results you have achieved or responsibility changes. For new jobs, you should create a new Career Inventory section and capture all the job information outlined in **Step 1**.

Keeping your Career Inventory updated will make it much easier to revise your resume or write a new one when you need to.

# Beyond the Winning Resume

By following the *7 Steps to a Winning Resume*, you have completed one of the most important parts of any job search. You should now have a resume that helps make your search successful. However, a resume is just one component of your job search.

To help with your LinkedIn profile, another important job search tool, you can download my *The 7 Steps LinkedIn Companion Guide* for free at http://www.BookHip.com/ZWNCPC.

For more job search advice, or if you need personalized help with writing your resume, visit my site at www.polarisresumes.com. The website has more resume tips, as well as information about my professional resume writing and job search coaching services.

If you liked this guide, please consider leaving a review at your book site of choice.

Good luck!

# About the Author

Carl is an international business executive and consultant with over twenty years of experience. Over the years, he has gained invaluable knowledge through working various jobs. From flipping burgers to jumping out of airplanes, to risk management consulting, to corporate planning at one of the largest companies in the world, Carl has a broad range of experience. He has earned an MA in International Relations from Yale University, an MBA from the University of Baltimore, and a BA from St. Olaf College.

Through his involvement in hiring people across multiple companies, as well as his personal job search experiences, Carl became dissatisfied with much of the available advice on how to write a resume and conduct an effective job search. This led him to become a Certified Professional Career Coach (CPCC) and Certified Professional Resume Writer (CPRW). Carl has worked as a freelance resume writer and job search coach for the last several years. *7 Steps to a Winning Resume* is the approach Carl developed to help people write their resumes. He currently provides professional resume and career search services through his website at www.polarisresumes.com.

www.ingramcontent.com/pod-product-compliance
Lightning Source LLC
Chambersburg PA
CBHW072148170526
45158CB00004BA/1556